THE BEST OF RILKE

THE BEST OF RILKE

TRANSLATED BY
WALTER ARNDT

FOREWORD BY
CYRUS HAMLIN

**72 FORM-TRUE VERSE TRANSLATIONS
WITH FACING ORIGINALS, COMMENTARY,
AND COMPACT BIOGRAPHY**

PUBLISHED FOR DARTMOUTH COLLEGE BY
UNIVERSITY PRESS OF NEW ENGLAND
HANOVER AND LONDON

UNIVERSITY PRESS OF NEW ENGLAND

BRANDEIS UNIVERSITY   DARTMOUTH COLLEGE
BROWN UNIVERSITY   UNIVERSITY OF NEW HAMPSHIRE
CLARK UNIVERSITY   UNIVERSITY OF RHODE ISLAND
UNIVERSITY OF CONNECTICUT   TUFTS UNIVERSITY
UNIVERSITY OF VERMONT

Arndt's translations of "Spring Fragment," "Before the Summer Rain,"
"The Poet," "Death of the Poet," "The Courtesan," and "The Island" were
first published in the *New England Review/Bread Loaf Quarterly* and are
reprinted with permission. "Intimation of Reality" ("Experience of Death")
appeared in *The Threepenny Review* and is reprinted with permission.

Excerpts from *Rilke: A Life* by Wolfgang Leppmann, translated by Russell
M. Stockman by permission of Fromm International Publishing Corpora-
tion. Copyright © 1984 by Fromm International Publishing Corporation.

Printed in the United States of America

∞

LIBRARY OF CONGRESS CATALOGING IN PUBLICATION DATA
Rilke, Rainer Maria, 1875–1926.
The best of Rilke.

Poems in English and German; commentary in English.
1. Rilke, Rainer Maria, 1875–1926—Translations, English.
I. Arndt, Walter W., 1916–   II. Title.
PT 2635.I65A224   1989   831'.912   88–40345
ISBN 0–87451–460–6
ISBN 0–87451–461–4 (pbk.)

5   4   3   2   I

To René Wellek and Helene Wolff,
youthful devotees of the living poet,
and Miriam Bach,
who acquired the taste

CONTENTS

CONTENTS

FOREWORD

Rainer Maria Rilke (1875–1926), master poet of Modernism in the German-speaking world, though he was born and raised in Prague and lived most of his adult life in self-imposed exile or continuous travels across most of Europe, achieved a singular status through his published work as an artist absolutely devoted to his poetry, even to the point where his life was subsumed by it. His reputation since his death has grown steadily among a readership which may now be considered worldwide, marked by frequent translations into various languages—English perhaps more than any other.

Rilke at his best is a poet's poet, and his mature poems are unsurpassed in the sense of mastery and consummate craftsmanship which they convey. Changes in critical taste over the years, especially during periods of radical politics —whether to the right or the left—have often judged Rilke to be too remote from reality or too esoteric for the general reader or too effete and refined for the issues which confront us today, especially among poets more engaged with issues of life and society than he would seem to be. Yet no other poet in any language, with the possible exception of William Butler Yeats (a near contemporary), can so perfectly represent that unique era of culture and art in the early years of this century in western Europe, which was just as remote and esoteric and effete as he was. Rilke is the supreme poet of a refined and sophisticated manner, a sensibility almost too painful in its intellectual and emotional subtleties, spokesman for a European culture now lost to us and removed even from access by the two world wars, the first of which he suffered through in a pained silence and the second of which he could never have imagined or survived. Nor can we easily sympathize any longer with the painful posturing of such an overly cultivated aesthetic selfhood, a kind of dandyism beyond the limits of decadence. His refinements were almost too extreme for the drawing rooms of his various wealthy patrons and friends, most of them women from the higher ranks of the nobility, who provided him with extended hospitality and support at places now associated with Rilke's name, such as Duino and Muzot, during those bittersweet dying years of the Belle Epoque. Was the city of Paris, center of modernism from the early years of the nineteenth century and home to so many of the precursors to Rilke in art and poetry, ever quite so perfect a resource for the visions of an aesthetic world view as that depicted in his *New Poems* of

1907/08? Despite the far greater notoriety of the elegies and sonnets which crown his last years, this book is the supreme achievement of Rilke's mature career and is a collection of poems almost equal in importance for the tradition of Modernism to Baudelaire's *Fleurs du Mal*. Most of the poems contained in this important new translation by Walter Arndt are taken from these *New Poems* in clear recognition of their unique importance for a modernist poetics. In these texts Rilke creates a complex world of oblique figurations, where every gesture and nuance contributes to the subtle tones and intricate rhythms of a high art.

The earliest of the poems included in the *Neue Gedichte* is dated by Ernst Zinn (editor of Rilke's *Saemtliche Werke*) early in 1903, possibly even at the end of 1902, and is the famous evocation of the caged panther, "Der Panther," which establishes a paradigm for Rilke's modernism. Also significant is the association of this poem with Paris (it was composed there, and the subheading locates the panther in the *Jardin des Plantes*), the artistic milieu which Rilke entered when he moved there earlier in that same year of 1902. Scholars of Rilke's work have long recognized the crucial importance for these *New Poems* of specific models and sources from the work of artists in France who are now identified with the era of Modernism. We think above all of the sculptor Rodin, for whom Rilke worked as private secretary and about whom he wrote an important monograph first drafted in 1905, and of the painter Cézanne, whose work the poet first encountered at an exhibition in Paris and about whom he wrote in a number of letters late in 1907. The first part of the *New Poems* has been referred to the sculpture of Rodin as model; the second part to the paintings of Cézanne. (These influences are surveyed by Brigitte Bradley in the introductions to her two volumes of interpretive readings devoted to this work: *R.M. Rilkes Neue Gedichte. Ihr zyklisches Gefüge* and *Rainer Maria Rilkes Der neuen Gedichte anderer Teil. Entwicklungsstufen seiner Pariser Lyrik*, Francke Verlag Berlin und Muenchen, 1967 & 1976.) More important for the craftsmanship of these poems, their style and verbal technique, and their acute sense of generic form, however, is the example of Baudelaire, whose *Les Fleurs du Mal* (according to Bradley, 1976, p. 6) was first recommended to Rilke by Rodin himself. A detailed study is still needed of the impact of Baudelaire on Rilke, specifically with regard to the *New Poems*, where the figurations of modernity may finally derive more from the language of Rilke's central precursor poet in his "Tableaux Parisiens" than from any actual experiences in the city itself, which both poets chose as the location and occasion for their poetry. It may yet be proved that the often flaunted notion of an objective poetics in the so-called *Dinggedichte* of Rilke should rather be referred to a complex intertextuality inspired by the careful study of Baudelaire.

A convenient focus for even a brief and tentative consideration of Rilke's poetics is provided by his appropriation of the sonnet as a traditional form of lyric from the singular use made of it in *Les Fleurs du Mal*. It should also be noted that Rilke wrote no sonnets at all prior to the *New Poems* and that the total number of sonnets in that collection (twenty-three and twenty-one, respectively, in the two parts) constitutes more than twenty percent of the whole. The proportion of sonnets in Baudelaire's collection is much higher, constituting just over forty percent of the whole (about sixty-five sonnets in all). Such statistics may not mean much as such, since numbers alone cannot account for a poet's conscious generic design. What matters more is the fact that Baudelaire seems to have been responsible singlehandedly for a serious revival of the sonnet in French literature after nearly two centuries of neglect. Rilke's rediscovery of the form could be attributed to a continuity of interest in it in German literature throughout the nineteenth century, starting with Goethe and the Romantics; yet no evidence exists, so far as I am aware, for any direct influence from German sources. Nor does it appear that Rilke's sonnets look back in any way to the conventions of Petrarch and the Renaissance tradition. For him the sonnet is a vehicle for a distinctly modernist poetics, for which I here propose that Baudelaire served as a virtually exclusive model. (When did Rilke first read Mallarmé? Presumably too late for any direct imitation at this stage of his career, even though the *Sonnets to Orpheus* are unthinkable without the example of the later Symbolist. By that time in 1922, however, Rilke's poetic craft had advanced into regions of its own unique creativity.)

What is it about the peculiar artifice and the limitations of form in the sonnet which made it so suitable for the poetry of modernism? Not the theme of love and all the associations inherited for such conventions from the example of Dante, Petrarch, and Shakespeare. When poets of so radical a modernity in German as Stefan George, Walter Benjamin and Paul Celan turn to the sonnets of such precursor poets as Dante, Shakespeare, and Baudelaire himself for exercises in poetic translation, it has nothing to do with traditional thematics. More to the point, especially for Rilke, is the implicit reflectivity of form which the sonnet imposes: a self-consciousness of craft at the level of the signifier. Not that the sonnet did not spawn across the centuries an entire sub-genre of poems about poetry, sonnets which address themselves *qua sonnet* to their own status as poems. Such auto-referential discourse—as in Wordsworth's "Scorn not the sonnet" or Goethe's "Natur und Kunst"—provides a heightened instance of a poetics in performance. The poem as formal statement also includes a reflective awareness of itself as thought in process. But Rilke is never so straightforward or obvious. His sonnets, as indeed his mature poems generally, never call attention to themselves as poetry at a thematic level, at least not prior to the *Duino Elegies*. Yet the medium of this poetry as language, above all in the complex and even programmatic use of formal devices of rhythmic phrasing and phonetic patterning, offers an implicit hermeneutics for that verbal medium. The language itself achieves a self-consciousness at the level of form which calls attention to itself merely through its versatility as *tour-de-force*. In this regard Baudelaire and Rilke are exemplary in their reflective mastery of the medium, though Baudelaire is perhaps more explicitly indebted to the thematics of the sonnet tradition than his German successor, while Rilke's subsequent practice in the *Sonnets to Orpheus* reestablished a fusion of thematics and form at a level of complexity and sophistication unsurpassed in the entire tradition of the sonnet.

A convenient programmatic focus for even a brief consideration of Rilke's poetics within the collection of *New Poems* is provided by the sonnets which introduce the two parts respectively, both of them dedicated to Apollo and both clearly intended to thematize the central problem of Rilke's art by invoking the ancient god of song through the example of his representations in works of sculpture as they survive in the modern world. We may surmise that the first of these Apollo sonnets, composed in July 1906, "Früher Apollo," was placed at the very outset of the collection in order to serve just such a programmatic purpose. Similarly, the later sonnet to Apollo, "Archaischer Torso Apollos," composed in the spring of 1908, was placed at the beginning of the second part explicitly as a companion text and as a kind of answer to the earlier sonnet which began the first part. The juxtaposition of these two poems will thus be instructive for purposes of comparison at several levels: from theme and form and subject to programmatic statement and even to the formulation of an implicit poetic theory. A few remarks on these two texts will also provide a representative sample of Rilke's work at its best and most characteristic and introduce a few thoughts about the challenge and the dilemma of translation.

Both sonnets employ the familiar fiction of an ecphrastic response to a statue of the god. Whether Rilke had a specific statue in mind for either instance—the one presumably a pre-Classical sculpture of Apollo, the other a fragment or torso without head or limbs (for both of which scholars have argued specific possible works)—may be of interest for a discussion of Rilke's manner of writing during his Paris period. Far more important for a reading of these poems, however, is the presumed model of art which Rilke here adopts from the tradition of aesthetics inherited from Winckelmann, Goethe and Hegel, where the Classical ideal of beauty in art would be embodied in sculpture (specifically ancient Greek sculpture), so that the human form serves to manifest an authentic sense of divinity as presence. The statue of Apollo—so Winckelmann had argued, for instance, in his famous evocation of the Apollo of Belvedere—truly reveals the god as immediate or identical to its embodiment in the stone, and—as Hegel argued in his *Aesthetics*, adapting the traditional Neo-Platonic notion of the work of art as the incarnation of spirit or the ideal—the human and the divine are perfectly fused in such a Classical statue. Rilke takes the premise of such an aesthetic ideal of epiphany for the sculpted form as a given or as an unspoken expectation, against which to measure the actual response to these particular examples of the god Apollo, neither of them capable, as it turns out, of fulfilling such expectations in a way which affirms such norms for the ideal of beauty without specific poetic problems. The one statue is too soon or too early for authentic revelation, premature in the process of cultural growth, though it is clearly perceived as anticipating the full presence of the god as yet to come; the other no longer can claim such revelatory power—or so it would at first appear—since only the mere ruin of such an ideal work still survives.

Such strategies of displacement, as if the Classical ideal of art were being subjected to the contingencies of history and occasion, shift the burden of signification away from the work itself toward the power of verbal response which the observer brings to it. That shift from what I would call the epiphanic to the hermeneutical mode corresponds to a shift in poetic or aesthetic theory, which Hegel defined in his *Aesthetics* as the contrast between what he called the Classical and the Symbolic or the Romantic (the one prior to and the other posterior to the Classical norm), a contrast also between the ancient and the modern and the shift from an aesthetics of presence to a consciousness of absence. Characteristically for Rilke's poetics, this movement also shifts the burden of signification away from the object of ecphrasis to the language of his own poetry as the medium of a hermeneutic response to that object. At the same time, in ways which are crucial for Rilke's use of poetic figures and verbal form, this shift also thematizes a principle of indirect or oblique mimesis, even to the point of negativity (in Hegel's sense of negating the negative), whereby the poem articulates a sense of what is *not* present or no longer can be, in the aesthetic object. Absence for vision thus becomes presence for the imagination through the mediating powers of poetic language. The implications of all this for Rilke's poetic craft and the implied program of his art in general will become apparent if we consider briefly some details from the texts of the two sonnets.

"Früher Apollo" evokes the statue of the god through a complex metaphor of the seasons—the transition from winter to spring or, more specifically, the anticipation of spring through the bright light of a winter morning—whereby the statue is compared with the branches of a tree, as yet without foliage, through which that light shines, indeed through which—as the poem asserts—"a morning shines which is already completely in spring." We may recognize that metaphorical *shining* to be identical with the idea of the work of art as the manifestation of divinity as presence; indeed, the play of Rilke's elaborate simile imposes such a model of presence upon the sense of a revealed light. "The god's head contains nothing that might keep the luster of all poems from striking us with almost lethal force"—like the arrows of the real god Apollo, whose epithet in Homer is "the one who strikes from afar." But Rilke's German phrase here, in a striking enjambment across the line break which separates the first from the second quatrain of the sonnet: ". . . der Glanz//Aller Gedichte. . . ," plays on a phonetic pattern of assonance and a rhythmic syncopation, in order to heighten the ambivalence of the term *Gedichte* as "poems," a sense which, if taken literally, would be absurd, yet within the metaphor of the god Apollo as the patron deity of art may be poetically perfect and exact. When applied ironically to the verbal medium of Rilke's sonnet as the source of the power, or "sheen" (*Glanz*), which is conveyed as a *seeing* in the visage of the statue (the *Schauen* of the god as yet without the shadow of laurel from his brow or, indeed, of any foliage at all), this verbal figure enables the reader of the poem to recognize how an imagined sense of the revealed divinity is here evoked despite its acknowledged absence.

A similar, yet opposite shift in the central metaphor of the face of the statue as tree occurs in the latter part of the sonnet through a temporal projection forward toward a later time, when that tree will sprout and blossom out of the eyebrows of the god [in "exalted branches"] "tall-stemmed" (*hochstaemmig*) as a "rose garden," from which the "leaves" or "petals" (*Blaetter*) will fall upon "the quivering of the mouth" (*des Mundes Beben*). Rilke's shifts and turns of figurative allusion move swiftly here, so that vision is transformed into oracle by a projection forward into an equally hypothetical and, for this statue, as yet unknown future. The figure of the rose garden in the face of the god yields these metaphorical *Blaetter*, which—by a hermeneutical displacement back upon the poem itself, exactly parallel to the earlier ambivalence of *Gedichte*—assume at least the possibility of referring to the text of the poem which we are reading as printed upon just such a *Blatt* (i.e., leaf or page). The oracle from the mouth of the god would thus be conveyed to us through such a leaf upon the trembling mouth, as if speech were to undergo a poetic transformation into the written text of the sonnet. But not quite yet: the rhetoric of the poem with its continuing elaboration of this single sentence through all fourteen lines reminds us that for now the mouth of the god is "still silent," "never used" (*niegebraucht*) and shining. And one last ironic twist of the figure that makes up this poem asserts that this mouth, which does not yet speak, merely smiles (*mit seinem Laecheln*) as if it were drinking in the substance of its future song (*sein Singen*). Through a brilliant reversal, signalled by the bold rhyme of past participles: *ausgelöst* and *eingeflößt*, Rilke concludes his sonnet with a sense of song—the song of the god Apollo, which is also implicitly the song to which this sonnet aspires—as being here received from a source which remains unexpressed and thus unknown, transcendent. As readers of "Früher Apollo," we need to refer the resonance of this metaphoric transformation back upon the poem itself in such a way that the statue of the god becomes the hypothetical subject, or source, for that as yet unheard and unknown song, which the poem is intended to signify or represent. Ultimately the challenge of meaning must fall upon ourselves as readers with regard to the complex strategy of figurative displacement whereby the poem conveys to us a sense of that which the statue of the god, at least this early statue of the god, cannot yet reveal. Vision becomes oracular speech or song only through imaginative negation, just as the source of the revealed light and the anticipated speech are displaced within the poem from the god to the statue to the text, that scene of language organized into a sonnet where finally for us as readers of Rilke the interplay of signifiers across the lines from rhyme to rhyme defines whatever we are able to make of it. Rilke thus throws down a challenge of competence or adequacy to his readers, which presumably we must share with the poet, in an effort to compensate by hermeneutic mediation for the power of divine presence which is evoked, figuratively displaced and finally denied by the language of the poem.

To read the later sonnet to Apollo as a programmatic companion text to the earlier requires a sense of contrast between a prior and a posterior model of vision, where the poem substitutes figurative reconstruction for anticipation. In place of an elaborate simile for future revelation we find the complex grammar of a subjunctive displacement. The crucial attribute of the god once again is his "gazing" (*Schauen*; the same verb was used in the earlier sonnet); but in the absence of the head on the torso that power of vision is asserted to be transposed, literally "screwed back" (*zurueckgeschraubt*) into the torso, like the wick on the kind of gas streetlamp called at that time a *candelabrum*, where it "sustains itself" (*sich haelt*) and "shines" (*glaenzt*, the same term used as a noun in the earlier sonnet: *Glanz*). Here also a movement is traced in "the quiet turning of the loins" (*im leisen Drehen der Lenden*), to which is attributed "a smile" (*ein Laecheln*; the same term again which was attributed to Apollo in the earlier sonnet). Yet all these qualities of the god as named in the torso sonnet are only the result of an implicit negation, attributed to the torso through an interpretive response by the observer. This interpretive process, however, is formulated as a projection upon the stone, as if it were an objective event caused by the effect of the stone on the observer. But the language of the poem gives it all away through a sequence of elaborate negatives in the subjunctive mood: "Sonst könnte nicht . . . und . . . könnte nicht . . . Sonst stünde dieser Stein entstellt . . . und . . . nicht . . . und nicht . . ." The ironic outcome of this verbal sequence is the assertion that the stone of the torso at all points of its surface *sees you*, which is also articulated in a statement with a double negative: "keine Stelle . . . die . . . nicht . . ." Crucial to this process of attribution are the active verbs describing what can only be understood as a figurative transformation of the static surface of the dead stone into a dynamic process of motion. The "eyeballs" (*Augenäpfel*, literally "eye-apples," alluding to the portrayal of the eyes in ancient sculpture as smooth curved surfaces) "ripened" (*reiften*), the torso "glows" (*glüht*), the bend or prow (*Bug*) of the breast "dazzles" (*blenden*), and the stone "shimmers" or "ripples" (*flimmerte*) and "breaks out" (*bräche . . . aus*). In addition to such dynamics of hypothetical activity three formal similes are superimposed, which identify the stone, respectively, with a "candelabrum" (*wie ein Kandelaber*), with "coats of wild beasts" (*wie Raubtierfelle*) and, finally, with a "star" (*wie ein Stern*). The reader of this sonnet needs to ask very carefully what the language is doing to the god.

Contrary to the mimetic relationships attributed in the survey of activities to the stone, the dynamics of the figures with which it is compared define a process of reflective cognition which reverses the relationship between the statue as object and the observer as subject. Instead of our looking at the statue, it looks at us; yet through such transformation of vision the poem finally thematizes an act of self-reflection. To have been screwed back into itself defines a form of internalization, which claims a life for the stone derived from the power of the god it makes—or made—manifest. The movement variously described as a bow or bending (*der Bug*), a turning (*Drehen*), a going (*gehen*) comes to focus on the crucial image of the sexual organs—which are also absent—as "that middle which bore the begetting" (*zu jener Mitte, die die Zeugung trug*). Without doing violence to the terms of this figure, we may also refer the entire line to the sonnet itself, which thematizes the sense of a center at the exact center of the sonnet (the final line of the octet), and also read the term for begetting as signifying "to bear witness" or even "to show" (*zeugen*, or even *zeigen*). Also complex and problematic is the image of the "fall" or "drop" of the shoulders (*der Schultern . . . Sturz*). Following evidence summoned about this image by Hermann J. Weigand, I take this term to signify more than the torso itself (both Winckelmann and Goethe are argued to have used *Sturz* as synonym for a torso in sculpture), since the word also designated in common usage a glass cover or belljar, which would literally be "transparent" (*durchsichtig*), through which one could see the object revealed which it covers and contains. What would thus be seen presumably is no less than the revealed presence of the god himself in and through the stone as a transparent embodiment of his light or power. The shimmering or rippling effect of the surface as of the coat of a beast of prey extends these metaphors of motion to yet a further degree of self-reflection. *Flimmern* would be the effect on the surface of the skin of a living animal caused by the movement of the muscles beneath: the cause of such movement is within, the effect is without. The stone of the torso is thus represented not only as if it were alive but explicitly as if it were motivated to move from within. The breaking out along the edges (*und bräche nicht aus allen seinen Raendern//aus*), finally, establishes a movement outward from the stone beyond the limits of the stone, so that an emanation of light is asserted to be perceived extending from it. The torso shines like a star. If again we may refer this figure back upon the poem itself through which it is articulated, such a simile would suggest both a limit to what may be signified and a transcendence of that limit. The ultimate achievement of the sonnet as utterance would thus be an epiphany of the divine. Yet given the focus of that event upon the response of the beholder, as a form of seeing which is equally a being seen, may we not also claim for such a moment of transcendence an implicit hermeneutics? The final line of the sonnet, perhaps as famous as any in all of Rilke, makes the implications of such a hermeneutics fully clear.

The reader of Rilke's sonnet must achieve a cognitive skill in ironic distancing, in order to liberate this sequence of radical metaphors from the control of the syntactical negatives that seem to ground everything stated by the sonnet in a sense of presence for the torso as an aesthetic object. Such a process of cognitive or hermeneutical reversal also enables us to refer the similes of the poem back upon the verbal medium itself as the vehicle of such radical figuration. For the language of the poem the stone of the statue must be recognized as the object which is *not* truly so as the sonnet describes it, but rather as the pretext of a divine power revealed as a transcendent otherness through the sequence of that radical figuration itself. More specifically, we may conclude that the images of seeing and illumination or epiphany, combined with the images of movement in so many different modes, above all involving the transference or crossing over or breaking out from an inside to an outside, may all serve to thematize the semiotic function of the language itself. The sonnet thus dramatizes an act of perception and response which resides in the sequence and interplay of the signifiers through phonetic and rhythmic patterns across the formal structure of rhyme and meter, to the point where we recognize as readers that the sense of the god as revealed through the archaic torso is actually the achievement exclusively of the language of the poem. This recognition as hermeneutical event may be thematized by the statement which concludes the poem: "You must change your life." Who says this and to whom? A straightforward, mimetically literal reading would perhaps refer this utterance to the torso—and thus by implication to the god as revealed through the torso—so that the stone thus achieves a voice of its own, as well as the capacity to look at us. It speaks to us with a call to change our lives rather in the manner of an oracle, appropriate to the tradition of Apollo at Delphi. At the same time, however, we cannot help but refer the statement equally to the poem itself as the concluding statement of the sonnet, rather like a motto or a refrain (since the last word of the poem, *ändern*, also rhymes—presumably not by accident —with *Rändern*), as if the voice of the poet as lyrical self and implied speaker of the poem were to assert this, specifically to himself in the rhetoric of a self-address. It is thus the appropriate hermeneutical outcome of the poet's observation of the torso and his transformation of that act of seeing through radical negation and figuration into an immediate response to the revealed presence of the god. But even that reading proves inadequate or insufficient, since finally we as readers of the sonnet must hear our own voice speaking these words, also as if to ourselves—the "you" thus becomes the self-reflective reader—in response to a reading of the poem as verbal event. Nor should there be any doubt that the change demanded in our life is anything other than the change already achieved and enacted in and through the language of the poem as a complex dialectic of figuration or verbal transformation at all levels: from stone to revealed divinity, from poem as text to articulated speech and vision, insight out of blindness, oracle out of silence, meaning out of negation, in accord with the latent generic form of the sonnet as it evolved throughout the tradition of its use from Dante, Petrarch, and Shakespeare to Baudelaire and Rilke himself.

How should a translator of Rilke attempt to convey some sense of such precise, yet oblique evocations? Much attention has been given in recent critical discussions from Benjamin to Derrida and beyond to theoretical issues, many of them daunting and insuperable, which arise whenever the question of translation is addressed. Yet no theory of translation will ever solve the immediate, practical dilemma of deciding on the right word at the right moment. Poetry is itself the outcome of a craft which is preeminently practical, and the translator of poetry, who perforce assumes a role subordinate to a text which is already fixed in its own unique language, must accommodate the craftsmanship of the translation to specific formal demands that are imposed from the original poem as a given. But Rilke's sonnets to Apollo offer perhaps some consolation in the testimony provided by the language in the poems concerning the challenge of evoking a sense of the god from those models of art external to the poems, the statues which themselves must be the source or occasion of any such evocation. A translation of either of these sonnets, for example into English, ought ideally to include a device like quotation marks around its own verbal performance to indicate that this text stands in relation to the original poem in a manner exactly parallel to the relation of Rilke's text to the hypothetical original statues of the god.

Rilke's poetics favors the verbal play of surfaces. Complexities of form at all levels assume a priority, often as if the poet's function in crafting the language of his poem extended no further than the versatility of such configurations. Yet the example of the Apollo sonnets shows clearly how the intricate figures of verbal form serve to compensate for a powerful sense of absence or distance or loss. In the face of an object perceived to be ineffable or even transcendent, the poem substitutes its own powers of fictive invention within the limits of its own verbal form, in order to evoke that sense of absence, distance or loss as the constitutive event for its own statement. The dilemma of a modernist aesthetics is thus displaced into the formal features of the verbal medium, the power of rhyme or the boldness of a rhythmic phrase, the shifts of syntax or the disruptions of grammar, similes which extend the limits of credibility, or the mere selection of words which evoke a transcendent surprise. In the face of such consummate verbal craft, what recourse can a translator have but to substitute equivalences that derive from a corresponding sense of verbal play? If Rilke can offer his sonnets as a substitute for the statues of the god, in such a way that the sonnets evoke the presence of the god more powerfully and more immediately than the statues ever could for him or for us, the translator of his poems must seek to convey some sense of a corresponding evocation through the language of his versions as substitutions for what in Rilke's German is acknowledged to be unique and inimitable. In effect, such a claim for translations must be impossible and even preposterous; yet the attempt must still be made. The strength of difference thus becomes the measure of success, so that ideally the translator of Rilke into English would assume a role corresponding to that of the poet himself, evoking as presence within the language of the poem what is acknowledged to be absent and beyond recovery. Has the challenge of translating authentic poetry ever been otherwise? Yet in the case of Rilke, particularly in these *New Poems*, for which the sonnets to Apollo stand as programmatic models, the poet himself defines the stance and sets the challenge which his translator must assume. The poem calls thematic attention to its unique achievement as text, even though that achievement is largely formal at various levels of language, as if to throw down a challenge for any translation: try to match this!

Walter Arndt meets this challenge with the benefit of his own distinctive experience and expertise in several languages across a distinguished career in translation. He has addressed the challenge of formal complexities in the poetry of Pushkin and in Goethe's *Faust*, not to mention the playful rhetoric of Wilhelm Busch or the surrealistic whimsy of Christian Morgenstern, which fully match the craft and subtle art of these *New Poems*. Yet in addition, as his own program notes and commentary to his versions of Rilke demonstrate, his translations also engage the specific challenge of these poems in direct, conscious response to the various attempts which precede him. Comparing translations of any poem by several translators can be a risky business. Can anyone claim an authority on all points in question? It has often been argued with conviction that great poetry assumes a life of its own which is continuous and ever renewed through a succession of readings from one generation to another. Yet the work of a translator is always contingent and specific to its own time and its own language. The best which any translation can hope to achieve is the best for here and now. Arndt's versions of Rilke recognize this limitation and, as the best translations always must, make a virtue of necessity, or at least they submit themselves willingly to the discourse of comparison, whereby readers are invited to an assessment similar to their own.

Rilke stands among the supreme poets of the modern tradition in Western literature, and the labor of finding adequate English versions will continue indefinitely. That labor must be regarded as a tribute to the poet as well as a service to his readers in the English-speaking world. But our judgment of the achievement of any published selection of poems by Rilke in English will tend to reflect the cumulative impact of the entire endeavor. In this regard the only significant competitor for this new translation by Walter Arndt would be the complete translation of the *New Poems*, the only previous attempt at prosodic accuracy, published by J.B. Leishman in 1964. Yet Leishman's versions of Rilke, however admirable the commitment and the dedication which stands behind them, does violence to English, besides being Edwardian in flavor and consistently disappointing in details. There have been other translations of uneven quality more recently—too many indeed of the *Duino Elegies* and the *Sonnets to Orpheus*, which Arndt has wisely avoided —but none in my view which can compete with this new selection. The singular achievement of Walter Arndt's new translation, which quite properly draws primarily on texts from the *New Poems*, may be defined at the level of poetic form. Arndt attends to the surface play of language in the complex patterns of rhythm and rhyme used by Rilke to a degree unequalled by any other translator into English. The outcome, of course, must be a sense of difference precisely at the level of the signifiers, yet that sense of difference, which we earlier argued to be a self-reflective function of Rilke's poetic forms that constitutes the poetics of his modernity, is clearly recognized by Arndt and often put to productive use for the challenge of translating what is often simply untranslatable. The poems contained in this collection are not of course the work of Rilke himself, but only versions in English of that work; yet the spirit of Rilke as poet, his manner, his quality, his style, comes across through Arndt with an authenticity and an immediacy that can only be achieved by a master translator on the basis of a lifetime of service to this essential, if always frustrating, cause. The achievement must be measured by the degree to which the frustration is resolved in the pleasure of the exercise itself, almost as if it were an act of original creation. The pleasure of these versions of Rilke is authentic, even if we also know that this sense of original creation is the product of the master translator's art.

December 1988   CYRUS HAMLIN
                                   Yale University

THE BEST OF RILKE

DER KNABE

Ich möchte einer werden so wie die,
die durch die Nacht mit wilden Pferden fahren,
mit Fackeln, die gleich aufgegangnen Haaren
in ihres Jagens großem Winde wehn.
Vorn möcht ich stehen wie in einem Kahne,
groß und wie eine Fahne aufgerollt.
Dunkel, aber mit einem Helm von Gold,
der unruhig glänzt. Und hinter mir gereiht
zehn Männer aus derselben Dunkelheit
mit Helmen, die, wie meiner, unstät sind,
bald klar wie Glas, bald dunkel, alt und blind.
Und einer steht bei mir und bläst uns Raum
mit der Trompete, welche blitzt und schreit,
und bläst uns eine schwarze Einsamkeit,
durch die wir rasen wie ein rascher Traum:
Die Häuser fallen hinter uns ins Knie,
die Gassen biegen sich uns schief entgegen,
die Plätze weichen aus: wir fassen sie,
und unsre Rosse rauschen wie ein Regen.

This is one of the relatively few items—half a dozen poems and two thematically closed cycles—chosen from the collection preceding Neue Gedichte, *which Rilke called* Das Buch der Bilder, *"The Book of Images." Its dates are 1902 and 1906. (The four-year hiatus between them is the time given in part to the strangely talentless* Stundenbuch, The Book of Hours, *a sad throwback to the mannered piety of Rilke's beginnings as a poet. Stundenbuch is embarrassingly intimate with the Almighty, seriously features a persona called "the pallid boy of blood," and presents its three cycles under a subtitle of archaic and pretentious solemnity: "comprising the three books, Of the Monkish Life / Of Pilgrimage / Of Poverty and Of Death.") This state of mind and taste, by the way, is clearly at work too in a famous piece of* Edelkitsch *of 1904/06/12, the best-selling* Lay of the Love and Death of the Cornet Christoph Rilke. *It was Rilke's personal late-adolescent response, marked by a highly stylized, purely gestural Christianity, to the still powerful pull of the decoratively idealized medievalism brought to the arts in the mid century by William Morris, Burne-Jones, the*

THE BOY

I want to be like one of those who race
With bolting steeds across the night-black air,
With flaming torches like unfastened hair
Aflutter in the stormwind of their chase.
I want to stand in front as on a prow,
Erect and slender like a banner scrolled,
Dark but accoutered in a helm of gold,
Which glitters restlessly; aback of me
Ten men, sprung from the same opacity,
In helms unsteadily aglint like mine,
Now clear as glass, now shaded, hoar, and blind.
And one stands next to me and blows us space
Out of a bugle's lips that scream and flare,
And blows black solitude, our thoroughfare,
Through which, as through a speeding dream, we race:
The houses in our wake drop to their knees,
There snake and skew towards us street and lane,
The squares that veer away from us we seize,
Our horses pelting on like sheets of rain.

*Rosettis, Boecklin—the Pre-Raphaelite infusion into decaying romanticism,
featuring Our (anorexic, chastely lilied) Lady of the sidelong gaze and the
bee-stung lips, hyper-active angels, prophets, monks, martyrs, pure damo-
zels, and saints. This retardation of Rilke's imagination and poetic practice
lasted till 1905 (his age thirty) and worried his friends. It is mentioned here
because echoes and whispers of it recur in the mature Rilke—see the
various cathedral poems in this volume.*

*The Boy consciously and sympathetically reproduces the excited stir-
rings of an entirely symbol-fed pre-adolescent imagination. It evokes, no
doubt from the poet's own not-so-distant past, the objectless verve, the
vague but powerful elation that German children and minds like Richard
Wagner derived from reading the Nibelungen Saga. It is in this puerile
sensibility that the impulse behind Rilke's* Cornet, *the dangerous fantasy
lives of Wihelm II and Theodore Roosevelt, and the Nazi phrase* heldisches
Leben—*a hero's life or heroic life style—have their origin.*

DIE KONFIRMANDEN

In weißen Schleiern gehn die Konfirmanden
tief in das neue Grün der Gärten ein.
Sie haben ihre Kindheit überstanden,
und was jetzt kommt, wird anders sein.

O kommt es denn! Beginnt jetzt nicht die Pause,
das Warten auf den nächsten Stundenschlag?
Das Fest ist aus, und es wird laut im Hause,
und trauriger vergeht der Nachmittag . . .

Das war ein Aufstehn zu dem weißen Kleide
und dann durch Gassen ein geschmücktes Gehn
und eine Kirche, innen kühl wie Seide,
und lange Kerzen waren wie Alleen,
und alle Lichter schienen wie Geschmeide,
von feierlichen Augen angesehn.

Und es war still, als der Gesang begann:
Wie Wolken stieg er in der Wölbung an
und wurde hell im Niederfall; und linder
denn Regen fiel er in die weißen Kinder.
Und wie im Wind bewegte sich ihr Weiß,
und wurde leise bunt in seinen Falten
und schien verborgne Blumen zu enthalten –:
Blumen und Vögel, Sterne und Gestalten
aus einem alten fernen Sagenkreis.

Und draußen war ein Tag aus Blau und Grün
mit einem Ruf von Rot an hellen Stellen.
Der Teich entfernte sich in kleinen Wellen,
und mit dem Winde kam ein fernes Blühn
und sang von Gärten draußen vor der Stadt.

Es war, als ob die Dinge sich bekränzten,
sie standen licht, unendlich leicht besonnt;
ein Fühlen war in jeder Häuserfront,
und viele Fenster gingen auf und glänzten.

FIRST COMMUNION

White-veiled, the first-communion children wade
Deep into gardens newly green with spring.
Here is deliverance from child's estate,
And what comes now will be a different thing.

Or will it? Isn't this just time's slow poise,
The wait for each new hour to toll out soon?
The feast run out, the house erupts in noise,
And there remains a drearier afternoon.

Oh what it was to rise to a gown of white,
Then pace in flowery state by lanes and mews,
And then a chapel, silken cool inside,
And tall thin tapers forming avenues;
And all the lights made sparks like clustered jewels
When solemn gazes gather up their sight.

And it was quiet when the chant began:
Cloudlike, it filtered up the vaulted span
And brightened as it fell; more mild and light
Than rain it sank amidst the girls in white,
So that their whiteness stirred as in a breeze
And gently took on hues in every fold,
And seemed to hide a flowery secret, hold
Blossoms and birds, and stars, and shapes untold
Out of some far-off hoary legend frieze.

It was a day in green and azure drafted,
With birdcall notes of red at lighted places;
The pond was rippling off to farther spaces,
And with the breeze a distant blooming wafted
And sang of gardens at the verge of town.

Things had adorned themselves with wreaths, it seemed,
They stood, ever so gently lit, and glowed;
From every housefront waves of feeling flowed,
And many windows opened up and gleamed.

PONT DU CARROUSEL

Der blinde Mann, der auf der Brücke steht,
Grau wie ein Markstein namenloser Reiche,
Er ist vielleicht das Ding, das immer gleiche,
Um das von fern die Sternenstunde geht,
Und der Gestirne stiller Mittelpunkt.
Denn alles um ihn irrt and rinnt und prunkt.

Er ist der unbewegliche Gerechte,
In viele wirre Wege hingestellt;
Der dunkle Eingang in die Unterwelt
Bei einem oberflächlichen Geschlechte.

PONT DU CARROUSEL

The blind man standing there upon the bridge,
Gray like a cairn of realms without a name,
He is perhaps that thing, that ever-same,
Which is the zodiac's quiet anchorage,
About which from afar the star hour spins;
For all around him strays and stirs and preens.

He is the ineradicable just one
Planted where many tangled pathways go,
The somber entrance to the world below
Among a populace of surface custom.

HERBSTTAG

Herr: es ist Zeit. Der Sommer war sehr groß.
Leg deinen Schatten auf die Sonnenuhren,
und auf den Fluren laß die Winde los.

Befiehl den letzten Früchten voll zu sein;
gieb ihnen noch zwei südlichere Tage,
dränge sie zur Vollendung hin und jage
die letzte Süße in den schweren Wein.

Wer jetzt kein Haus hat, baut sich keines mehr.
Wer jetzt allein ist, wird es lange bleiben,
wird wachen, lesen, lange Briefe schreiben
und wird in den Alleen hin und her
unruhig wandern, wenn die Blätter treiben.

AUTUMN DAY

Lord: it is time. Great was the summer's feast.
Now lay upon the sun-dials your shadow
And on the meadows have the winds released.

Command the last of fruits to round their shapes;
Grant two more days of south for vines to carry,
To their perfection thrust them on, and harry
The final sweetness into heavy grapes.

Who has not built his house, will not start now.
Who now is by himself will long be so,
Be wakeful, read, write lengthy letters, go
In vague disquiet pacing up and down
Denuded lanes, with leaves adrift below.

ABEND

Der Abend wechselt langsam die Gewänder,
die ihm ein Rand von alten Bäumen hält;
du schaust: und von dir scheiden sich die Länder,
ein himmelfahrendes und eins, das fällt;

und lassen dich, zu keinem ganz gehörend,
nicht ganz so dunkel wie das Haus, das schweigt,
nicht ganz so sicher Ewiges beschwörend
wie das, was Stern wird jede Nacht und steigt—

und lassen dir (unsäglich zu entwirrn)
dein Leben bang und riesenhaft und reifend,
so dass es, bald begrenzt und bald begreifend,
abwechselnd Stein in dir wird und Gestirn.

Rilke's Book of Images *is an uneven collection which juxtaposes some of*
the painfully affected, almost born-again products of his art nouveau *period*
of the nineties with some of the highly disciplined, gleaming "object poems"
characteristic of the best of Neue Gedichte. *"Evening" may be thought of*
as a hybrid, leaning both backward and forward. "Disciplined," of course,
does not mean strained or metallic. The wonderfully lax and accomplished
two opening lines combine the dreamy legato rhythm which Rilke masters
so easily, when not too earnest, with a charmingly domestic double
metaphor: evening slowly changing its robes, assisted (we see in after-image)
by a fringe of ancient trees which hold them out like a lady's maid.
But even as early as this, the fine concreteness of Rilke's new verse
begins to crumble. The sky-bright upper raiment, plausibly enough, turns
into a heaven-bound realm; the lower zone of the tree fringe "falls," rela-
tively, and shrinks into the darkening earth. But inadvertently, the two

EVENING

The evening is slowly changing garb,
Held for it by a fringe of old tree-tops;
Before your eyes, the territories part,
One that ascends to heaven, one that drops;

And leave you fully congruent with neither—
Not quite as lightless as the silent house,
Nor as assuredly boding last things, either,
As what turns into star each night and mounts—

And leave to you (quite hopeless to unsnarl)
Your life uneasy, vast, to ripeness tending,
So that it, now confined, now comprehending,
Turns now to stone within you, now to star.

lightly tinted hemispheres of the evening sky have now turned into portentous "lands which sever before you" and tend to oust you from either habitat, leaving you "not quite as dark as the silent house" nor "quite so surely adjuring [incanting, conjuring up] eternal things as that [i.e., the sky-bound realm] which becomes star each night and rises . . ." Unsorted bowels of poetry which few haruspices could make sense of!

This ballooning of the original image has caused both the poem's identity and the thinning semantic sinews to part. Next, the partial rejection from both "lands," it is suggested, leave the observer's life (by a process rightly called "hopeless to unravel") "uneasy, gigantic, and maturing" (not unlike an overripe pumpkin), so that "now limited and now comprising," it alternates in him between "star and stone." The poem has collapsed in bombastic vagueness perilously close, here and there, to the ludicrous. Its end is a stranger to its slight but gifted beginning.

DIE HEILIGEN DREI KÖNIGE

Legende

Einst als am Saum der Wüsten sich
auftat die Hand des Herrn
wie eine Frucht, die sommerlich
verkündet ihren Kern,
da war ein Wunder: Fern
erkannten und begrüßten sich
drei Könige und ein Stern.

Drei Könige von Unterwegs
und der Stern Überall,
die zogen alle (überlegs!)
so rechts ein Rex und links ein Rex
zu einem stillen Stall.

Was brachten die nicht alles mit
zum Stall von Bethlehem!
Weithin erklirrte jeder Schritt,
und der auf einem Rappen ritt,
saß samten und bequem.
Und der zu seiner Rechten ging,
der war ein goldner Mann,
und der zu seiner Linken fing
mit Schwung und Schwing
und Klang und Kling
aus einem runden Silberding,
das wiegend und in Ringen hing,
ganz blau zu rauchen an.
Da lachte der Stern Überall
so seltsam über sie,
und lief voraus und stand am Stall
und sagte zu Marie:

Da bring ich eine Wanderschaft
aus vieler Fremde her.
Drei Könige mit Magenkraft
von Gold und Topas schwer
und dunkel, tumb und heidenhaft, —
erschrick mir nicht zu sehr.
Sie haben alle drei zu Haus

ADVENT OF THE MAGI

A Legend

Time was when at the desert's verge
The Lord's hand opened wide,
As when a fruit at summer's urge
Proclaims its kernel's pride;
Then passed a wonder: from afar
There met and halted side by side
Three monarchs and a star.

Three monarchs, come from Dayandnight,
And All-Above the star
Betook themselves (the drollest sight,
A Rex at left, a Rex at right)
Unto a silent barn.

What-all they had not brought with them
To take to Bethlehem!
Such clink and clangor ringed their course,
And he who rode the sable horse
Sat velvet-snug and tight,
And he who walked upon his right
All cased in gold he went;
The one at left held up a sling
And, rung and ring,
And swung and swing,
From out a rounded silver thing
That hung in chains of ring-in-ring,
He drew a blue blue scent.

Then laughed the star named All-Above
So strange a laugh at them,
And ran ahead to Bethlehem
And said to Mary: "Love,
I'm bringing you a pilgrimage
Outlandish as can be,
Three kings endowed with might and rich
In gold and jewelry,
All dark and dull and heathenish—
But don't you faint on me!
They have at home, each of the three,

zwölf Töchter, keinen Sohn,
so bitten sie sich deinen aus
als Sonne ihres Himmelblaus
und Trost für ihren Thron.
Doch mußt du nicht gleich glauben: Bloß
ein Funkelfürst und Heidenscheich
sei deines Sohnes Los.
Bedenk, der Weg ist groß.
Sie wandern lange, Hirten gleich,
inzwischen fällt ihr reifes Reich
weiß Gott wem in den Schoß.
Und während hier, wie Westwind warm,
der Ochs ihr Ohr umschnaubt,
sind sie vielleicht schon alle arm
und so wie ohne Haupt.

Drum mach mit deinem Lächeln licht
die Wirrnis, die sie sind,
und wende du dein Angesicht
nach Aufgang und dein Kind;
dort liegt in blauen Linien,
was jeder dir verließ:
Smaragda und Rubinien
und die Tale von Türkis.

Twelve daughters and no son;
So they request your son from you
For sunshine in their heaven's blue
And solace for their throne.
But don't you fear, for Heaven's sake,
A spangled prince or pagan sheik
Might be your baby's lot:
Their way is long and hot,
And shepherd-like they rove and roam
While back at home
Their ripe domains by guile or doom
Fall unto God knows whom.
While in this barn, warm as the West,
The ox snuffs up their hair,
They may all three be dispossessed
And headless, like, out there.

So brighten, Mary, with thy smile
The turmoil that they are,
And turn thy countenance's star
To Orient, and thy child;
There lies in azure tracery
What each gave up for thee:
Smaraghdad and Rubinia
And the vales of Saphiry.

DIE STIMMEN

TITELBLATT

Die Reichen und Glücklichen haben gut schweigen,
niemand will wissen, was sie sind.
Aber die Dürftigen müssen sich zeigen,
müssen sagen: ich bin blind,
oder: ich bin im Begriff es zu werden
oder: es geht mir nicht gut auf Erden,
oder: ich habe ein krankes Kind,
oder: da bin ich zusammengefügt . . .

Und vielleicht, daß das gar nicht genügt.

Und weil alle sonst, wie an Dingen,
an ihnen vorbeigehn, müssen sie singen.

Und da hört man noch guten Gesang.

Freilich die Menschen sind seltsam; sie hören
lieber Kastraten in Knabenchören.

Aber Gott selber kommt und bleibt lang,
wenn ihn diese Beschnittenen stören.

VOICES

FRONTISPIECE

The rich and happy are safe in their shells,
No one asks questions of their kind.
The derelicts, though, must exhibit themselves,
Have to say: I am blind,
Or about to be,
Or Life on earth is not kind to me,
Or I've an ailing child,
Or Here's where I am patched or spliced . . .

And even these may not suffice.

And since their like is overlooked, like a thing,
They must sing.

You sometimes hear a pretty good song.

Most, to be sure, would prefer to hear
Castrates in boys' choirs. People are queer.

But God will come by, and stay quite long
When this kind of eunuch troubles His ear.

DAS LIED DES BETTLERS

Ich gehe immer von Tor zu Tor,
verregnet und verbrannt;
auf einmal leg ich mein rechtes Ohr
in meine rechte Hand.
Dann kommt mir meine Stimme vor,
als hätt ich sie nie gekannt.

Dann weiß ich nicht sicher, wer da schreit,
ich oder irgendwer.
Ich schreie um eine Kleinigkeit.
Die Dichter schrein um mehr.

Und endlich mach ich noch mein Gesicht
mit beiden Augen zu;
wie's dann in der Hand liegt mit seinem Gewicht,
sieht es fast aus wie Ruh.
Damit sie nicht meinen, ich hätte nicht,
wohin ich mein Haupt tu.

THE BEGGAR'S SONG

I keep on going from door to door,
Rained on and tanned.
Abruptly I cradle my right ear
In my right hand.
Then my song begins to sound quite queer,
As if never heard before.

Then I can't quite tell
If it's me that is crying or
Whoever . . . I cry for a bagatelle;
The poets cry for more.

I may end up shuttering out all space,
See my lids instead;
As my palm then bears the weight of my face
It's almost a bed.
Lest people think I have no place
Where to rest my head.

DAS LIED DES BLINDEN

Ich bin blind, ihr draußen, das ist ein Fluch,
ein Widerwillen, ein Widerspruch,
etwas täglich Schweres.
Ich leg meine Hand auf den Arm der Frau,
meine graue Hand auf ihr graues Grau,
und sie führt mich durch lauter Leeres.

Ihr rührt euch und rückt und bildet euch ein,
anders zu klingen als Stein auf Stein,
aber ihr irrt euch: ich allein
lebe und leide und lärme.
In mir ist ein endloses Schrein,
und ich weiß nicht, schreit mir mein
Herz oder meine Gedärme.

Erkennt ihr die Lieder? Ihr sanget sie nicht,
nicht ganz in dieser Betonung.
Euch kommt jeden Morgen das neue Licht
warm in die offene Wohnung.
Und ihr habt ein Gefühl von Gesicht zu Gesicht,
und das verleitet zur Schonung.

THE BLIND MAN'S SONG

I am blind, you out there, it's a cross I bear,
A paradox and a sick despair,
A doom that has cloyed.
The woman is at my side, I lay
My gray hand onto her gray-in-gray,
And she leads me through nothing but void.

You stir, you defer, and you seem to think
Your sound is more than a stony clink,
but you're wrong: it is I alone
Who is and who aches and yells out vowels.
Within me there is an endless groan,
And I cannot tell if it is the moan
Of my heart or my bowels.

Do my songs ring a bell? You never sang those,
Not quite with the same innuendos . . .
For you each morning the warm light flows
Afresh through your open windows.
There's awareness for you between face and face,
Which fosters a sparing grace.

DAS LIED DES TRINKERS

Es war nicht in mir. Es ging aus und ein.
Da wollt ich es halten. Da hielt es der Wein.
(Ich weiß nicht mehr, was es war.)
Dann hielt er mir jenes und hielt mir dies,
bis ich mich ganz auf ihn verließ.
Ich Narr.

Jetzt bin ich in seinem Spiel, und er streut
mich verächtlich herum und verliert mich noch
an dieses Vieh, an den Tod.   [heut
Wenn der mich, schmutzige Karte, gewinnt,
so kratzt er mit mir seinen grauen Grind
und wirft mich fort in den Kot.

THE DRUNKARD'S SONG

It wasn't inside me. I'd find it and lose it.
I tried to hang on to it then. And booze it.
(I forget what it was.)
Then booze did now this, now that for me,
And I came to depend on it totally.
Fool that I was.

Now I'm part of its game, and it flings me about
With contempt, and before the month is out
Will lose me to Death, that thug.
When I'm won by him, a grimy old trey,
He'll scratch his gray scab-face with me
And toss me into the muck.

DAS LIED DES SELBSTMÖRDERS

Also noch einen Augenblick.
Daß sie mir immer wieder den Strick
zerschneiden.
Neulich war ich so gut bereit,
und es war schon ein wenig Ewigkeit
in meinen Eingeweiden.

Halten sie mir den Löffel her,
diesen Löffel Leben.
Nein, ich will und ich will nicht mehr,
laßt mich mich übergeben.

Ich weiß, das Leben ist gar und gut,
und die Welt ist ein voller Topf,
aber mir geht es nicht ins Blut,
mir steigt es nur zu Kopf.

Andere nährt es, mich macht es krank;
begreift, daß man's verschmäht.
Mindestens ein Jahrtausendlang
brauch ich jetzt Diät.

THE SUICIDE'S SONG

So it's back once more, back up the slope.
Why do they always ruin my rope
With their cuts?
I felt so ready the other day,
Had a real foretaste of eternity
In my guts.

Spoonfeeding me yet another sip
From life's cup.
I don't want it, won't take any more of it,
Let me throw up.

Life is medium rare and good, I see,
And the world full of soup and bread,
But it won't pass into the blood for me,
Just goes to my head.

It makes me ill, though others it feeds;
Do see that I must deny it!
For a thousand years from now at least
I'm keeping a diet.

DAS LIED DES IDIOTEN

Sie hindern mich nicht. Sie lassen mich gehn.
Sie sagen, es könne nichts geschehn.
Wie gut.
Es kann nichts geschehn. Alles kommt und kreist
immerfort um den Heiligen Geist,
um den gewissen Geist (du weißt)—,
wie gut.

Nein, man muß wirklich nicht meinen, es sei
irgend eine Gefahr dabei.
Das ist freilich das Blut.
Das Blut ist das Schwerste. Das Blut ist schwer.
Manchmal glaub ich, ich kann nicht mehr—.
(Wie gut.)

Ah, was ist das für ein schöner Ball;
rot und rund wie ein Überall.
Gut, daß ihr ihn erschuft.
Ob der wohl kommt, wen man ruft?

Wie sich das alles seltsam benimmt,
ineinandertreibt, auseinanderschwimmt:
freundlich, ein wenig unbestimmt.
Wie gut.

THE IDIOT'S SONG

They leave me in peace, don't get in my way.
They say nothing can happen, I'll be O.K.
How nice.
Nothing can happen. All comes and is tossed
In circles around the Holy Ghost,
That certain ghost (you know, of course)—
How nice.

No one should really get the idea
There's any danger here.
Of course there is blood.
Blood is the heaviest. Blood's a ton.
Sometimes I feel that I can't go on—
(How nice).

Look, what a beautiful ball out there;
Red and round like an Everywhere.
Good thing you made that ball.
Will it come if I call?

How all these things seem a little kinked,
Drifting together, becoming unlinked:
Friendly; just a bit indistinct.
How nice.

DAS LIED DER WAISE

Ich bin Niemand und werde auch Niemand sein.
Jetzt bin ich ja zum Sein noch zu klein;
aber auch später.

Mütter und Väter,
erbarmt euch mein.

Zwar es lohnt nicht des Pflegens Müh:
ich werde doch gemäht.
Mich kann keiner brauchen: jetzt ist es zu früh
und morgen ist es zu spät.

Ich habe nur dieses eine Kleid,
es wird dünn und es verbleicht,
aber es hält eine Ewigkeit
auch noch vor Gott vielleicht.

Ich habe nur dieses bißchen Haar
(immer dasselbe blieb),
das einmal Eines Liebstes war.

Nun hat er nichts mehr lieb.

THE ORPHAN'S SONG

I'm no one, and that's what I'll always stay.
I'm too little to *be* yet, anyway;
But later too.

Mothers and fathers, you
Take pity on me.

Not that caring for me would pay.
My fate will beckon.
I don't come in handy: too early one day,
Too late the second.

I have only this in the way of clothes;
It's faded and worn, but will do
Perhaps a small eternity through,
Right up to God's throne; who knows.

I've only this bit of hair; not much,
But still the same, somehow.
It was someone's favorite thing to touch.

But he loves nothing now.

DAS LIED DER WITWE

Am Anfang war mir das Leben gut.
Es hielt mich warm, es machte mir Mut.
Daß es das allen Jungen tut,
wie konnt ich das damals wissen.
Ich wußte nicht, was das Leben war—,
auf einmal war es nur Jahr und Jahr,
nicht mehr gut, nicht mehr neu, nicht mehr
wie mitten entzwei gerissen.   [wunderbar,

Das war nicht seine, nicht meine Schuld;
wir hatten beide nichts als Geduld,
aber der Tod hat keine.
Ich sah ihn kommen (wie schlecht er kam),
und ich schaute ihm zu, wie er nahm und nahm:
es war ja gar nicht das Meine.

Was war denn das Meine; Meines, Mein?
War mir nicht selbst mein Elendsein
nur vom Schicksal geliehn?
Das Schicksal will nicht nur das Glück,
es will die Pein und das Schrein zurück,
und es kauft für alt den Ruin.

Das Schicksal war da und erwarb für ein Nichts
jeden Ausdruck meines Gesichts
bis auf die Art zu gehn.
Das war ein täglicher Ausverkauf,
und als ich leer war, gab es mich auf
und ließ mich offen stehn.

THE WIDOW'S SONG

Life was good to me when I was a bride,
It kept me warm and it took my side.
That it gives all the young that free ride,
How could I think that true?
I hadn't a clue what life was then . . .
All at once, it was just year-out, year-in,
Never good, never new, never great again,
As if torn right in two.

Neither he nor I was to blame, or bad;
Patience was all the two of us had,
But death has none at all.
I saw him come (how shabby his look),
And I looked on as he took and took:
It wasn't mine, after all.

What was mine, my own, what belonged to me?
Hadn't fate even lent me my misery
For a one-night stand?
Fate won't reclaim only happiness,
It has anguish and screaming to repossess,
Buys ruin up second-hand.

Fate was right there, bought me up for a song,
Down to the way I walk along,
Every last expression I wear.
All had to go, as brisk as could be,
And when I ran out it gave up on me
And left me gutted there.

DAS LIED DES ZWERGES

Meine Seele ist vielleicht grad und gut;
aber mein Herz, mein verbogenes Blut,
alles das, was mir wehe tut,
kann sie nicht aufrecht tragen.
Sie hat keinen Garten, sie hat kein Bett,
sie hängt an meinem scharfen Skelett
mit entsetztem Flügelschlagen.

Aus meinen Händen wird auch nichts mehr.
Wie verkümmert sie sind: sieh her:
zähe hüpfen sie, feucht und schwer,
wie kleine Kröten nach Regen.
Und das Andere an mir ist
abgetragen und alt und trist;
warum zögert Gott, auf den Mist
alles das hinzulegen.

Ob er mir zürnt für mein Gesicht
mit dem mürrischen Munde?
Es war ja so oft bereit, ganz licht
und klar zu werden im Grunde;
aber nichts kam ihm je so dicht
wie die großen Hunde.
Und die Hunde haben das nicht.

THE DWARF'S SONG

My soul may be straight and plane,
But my heart, my contorted veins,
All else that is giving me pain—
My soul can't uphold these things.
It has no garden or bed it owns,
It hangs on my jagged crate of bones
With a horrified beating of wings.

Nor will my hands ever get me far.
Just look how stunted they are.
They heave and twitch, dankly bizarre,
Like small toads, rain-slick and plump.
Nor's the rest of me in better state,
All threadbare and sad and third-rate;
Why does the good Lord hesitate
To toss it on the dump?

Is he angry with me because of the sight
Of my face with its scowl?
It wanted so often to turn all bright
And clear right down to the soul,
Yet nothing ever came close, skin-tight,
But the big dogs, who growl;
And the dogs don't have it right.

DAS LIED DES AUSSÄTZIGEN

Sieh, ich bin einer, den alles verlassen hat.
Keiner weiß in der Stadt von mir.
Aussatz hat mich befallen.
Und ich schlage mein Klapperwerk,
klopfe mein trauriges Augenmerk
in die Ohren allen,
die nahe vorübergehn.
Und die es hölzern hören, sehn
erst gar nicht her, und was hier geschehn,
wollen sie nicht erfahren.

Soweit der Klang meiner Klapper reicht,
bin ich zuhause; aber vielleicht
machst du meine Klapper so laut,
dass sich keiner in meine Ferne traut,
der mir jetzt aus der Nähe weicht.
Sodaß ich sehr lange gehen kann,
ohne Mädchen, Frau oder Mann
oder Kind zu entdecken.

Tiere will ich nicht schrecken.

To the twentieth-century reader of normal sensibility and social compassion
—all but the American "yuppy" of the 1980s and the generations of pluto-
crats who bred him—the gallery of "insulted and injured" (Dostoevsky)
presented in Rilke's cycle Voices would be an obvious and powerful, if
understated, argument for social remedy and reform. Rilke, on the other
hand, arch-reactionary in these matters, saw an esthetic rightness in pov-
erty and inequality, decried interference with established misery for better-
ment's sake, and subscribed to the medieval motto "God bless the squire
and his relations, and keep us in our proper stations." This callous Bourbon
cast of mind, suspected by few of his friends and probably connected with
his lifelong craving for aristocratic roots and ties, is discernible already in
relatively early works like the Prague tales, Stories of Our Lord, and Of
Poverty and of Death. Answering a journalistic questionnaire thirty years
later, far from revising his relish of inequality, he kneaded his sentiments
into a miniature social theory:

> people would be mistaken to allocate any of my strivings to this category
> [of social concern]. An element of human sympathy, of fraternal feeling

THE LEPER'S SONG

Look, I am one abandoned by all.
No one in town knows about me.
I have been stricken by leprosy.
And I work this rattle-thing,
Drumming the sorry sensation I bring
To the ears of all
Who pass close in.
And those who hear its wooden ring
Won't even look what is happening,
They don't want to know.

As far and wide as my rattle raps
I feel at home; but perhaps
You make my rattle so loud and strange
That none dare enter my distant range
Who now ignore me close by;
So I may go a very long span
And never encounter woman or man
On the way, or child.

I won't drive animals wild.

comes naturally to me, to be sure, and must be rooted in my being. . . . But what totally distinguishes such a cheerful and natural attention from "social concern," as people understand it, is a complete disinclination, even distaste, for changing anyone's situation, or, as the saying goes, improve it. No one's situation in the world is such that it could not be of peculiar benefit to his soul. If at some point I was able to cast the imaginary voices of the dwarf or the beggar into the mold of my heart, the metal of this casting was not derived from the wish that the dwarf's or the beggar's lot might be lightened; on the contrary, only exaltation of their incomparable fates enabled the poet, in his abrupt resolve to treat them, to be veracious and thorough, and he had to fear and decline nothing more than a corrected world in which the dwarves are elongated and the beggars enriched. The god of plenitude sees to it that these variants do not cease, and it would be the shallowest of interpretations were one to take the poet's enjoyment of this suffering multiplicity for an esthetic alibi . . .

AUS EINER STURMNACHT

TITELBLATT

Die Nacht, vom wachsenden Sturme bewegt,
wie wird sie auf einmal weit, —
als bliebe sie sonst zusammengelegt
in die kleinlichen Falten der Zeit.
Wo die Sterne ihr wehren, dort endet sie nicht
und beginnt nicht mitten im Wald
und nicht an meinem Angesicht
und nicht mit deiner Gestalt.
Die Lampen stammeln und wissen nicht:
lügen wir Licht?
Ist die Nacht die einzige Wirklichkeit
seit Jahrtausenden . . .

FROM A STORMY NIGHT

TITLE PAGE

The night, by the rising storm bestirred,
How spacious it suddenly seems—
As though at other times it were shirred
Between time's pedantic seams.
Where the stars would bar it, it does not wane,
Nor wax from the forest glens;
Nor at my face begin its reign
Nor at your lineaments.
The lanterns stammer and have to ask
Do we feign our light?
Has the only real thing for millennia past
Been the night?

In solchen Nächten kannst du in den Gassen
Zukünftigen begegnen, schmalen blassen
Gesichtern, die dich nicht erkennen
und dich schweigend vorüberlassen.
Aber wenn sie zu reden begännen,
wärst du ein Langevergangener,
wie du da stehst,
langeverwest.
Doch sie bleiben im Schweigen wie Tote,
obwohl sie die Kommenden sind.
Zukunft beginnt noch nicht.
Sie halten nur ihr Gesicht in die Zeit
und können, wie unter Wasser, nicht schauen;
und ertragen sie's doch eine Weile,
sehn sie wie unter den Wellen: die Eile
Von Fischen und das Tauchen von Tauen.

I

In such nights you're apt to come upon
Future ones along the sidewalks—peaked and wan
Visages which do not take you in,
Let you pass in silence and go on.
Mark, though: were they to begin
Speaking, you would be defunct, forgotten
As you stand there,
Long since rotten.
Yet they remain in silence, like the dead,
For all they are the coming ones.
The future hasn't yet begun.
They only hold their faces into time
But cannot really look, as though submerged;
And if they do endure it for a while,
They see as under waves: a darting file
Of fishes and the slant of ropes immersed.

In solchen Nächten gehn die Gefängnisse auf.
Und durch die bösen Träume der Wächter
gehn mit leisem Gelächter
die Verächter ihrer Gewalt.
Wald! Sie kommen zu dir, um in dir zu schlafen,
mit ihren langen Strafen behangen.
Wald!

2

Such nights may see the opening of the jails,
When through the turnkeys' haunted dreams
Walk with hushed gales, soft screams
Of laughter those who scorn their power.
Forest! They seek your trees to sleep among,
With their long sentences hung.
     Forest!

3

In solchen Nächten ist auf einmal Feuer
in einer Oper. Wie ein Ungeheuer
beginnt der Riesenraum mit seinen Rängen
Tausende, die sich in ihm drängen,
zu kauen.
Männer und Frauen
staun sich in den Gängen,
und wie sich alle aneinander hängen,
bricht das Gemäuer, und es reißt sie mit.
Und niemand weiß mehr, wer ganz unten litt;
während ihm einer schon das Herz zertritt,
sind seine Ohren noch ganz voll von Klängen,
die dazu hingehn . . .

3

In such nights of a sudden fires break out
In opera houses. Like a saurian snout
The monstrous horseshoe with its rows and tiers
Begins to chew the throngs pent in its den.
Women and men,
Choking in lobbies, smothered between piers,
Pile up into a welded human mound
Till bursting masonry cascades them down.
Who knows who drew the dreadful downmost part;
When someone has already crushed his heart,
His ears are still awash with sound
Making for it . . .

4

In solchen Nächten, wie vor vielen Tagen,
fangen die Herzen in den Sarkophagen
vergangner Fürsten wieder an zu gehn:
und so gewaltig drängt ihr Wiederschlagen
gegen die Kapseln, welche widerstehn,
daß sie die goldnen Schalen weitertragen
durch Dunkel und Damaste, die zerfallen.
Schwarz schwankt der Dom mit allen seinen Hallen.
Die Glocken, die sich in die Türme krallen,
hängen wie Vögel, bebend stehn die Türen,
und an den Trägern zittert jedes Glied:
als trügen seinen gründenden Granit
blinde Schildkröten, die sich rühren.

4

In such nights, as they did in times gone by,
The hearts within the sealed sarcophagi
Of erstwhile princes start to beat again:
And with such power their livened pulses pound
Against the body-casks—which stand their ground—
That they propel the golden capsules then
Through gloom and damask cloth that gives and frays.
The minster, naves and transept, blackly sways.
The bells, which clawed for holds among their stays,
Hang there like birds at bay, the doors mismate,
And on the pillars every strut is clenched
As if its founding granite plates were wrenched
By blind sea-turtles shifting place and weight.

5

In solchen Nächten wissen die Unheilbaren:
wir waren . . .
Und sie denken unter den Kranken
einen einfachen guten Gedanken
weiter, dort, wo er abbrach.
Doch von den Söhnen, die sie gelassen,
geht der jüngste vielleicht in den einsamsten Gassen;
denn gerade diese Nächte
sind ihm, als ob er zum erstenmal dächte:
Lange lag es über ihm bleiern,
abert jetzt wird sich alles entschleiern, —
und daß er das feiern wird,
      fühlt er . . .

5

In such nights the incurable see:
we will not be . . .
And they resume among the ill
a simple thought of good will
from the place it broke off.
But of the sons they raise
the youngest may walk the loneliest ways;
for just these nights
make him feel he is thinking for the first time:
He's long lain under a leaden pall,
but here comes what will lift the thrall—
and that he will celebrate it all,
        he senses . . .

In solchen Nächten sind alle die Städte gleich,
alle beflaggt.
Und an den Fahnen vom Sturm gepackt
und wie an Haaren hinausgerissen
in irgendein Land mit ungewissen
Umrissen und Flüssen.
In allen Gärten ist dann ein Teich,
an jedem Teiche dasselbe Haus,
in jedem Hause dasselbe Licht;
und alle Menschen sehn ähnlich aus
und halten die Hände vorm Gesicht.

6

In such nights, all cities are alike,
Alive with flags,
Caught in the storm by the whipping rags
And dragged away as if by the hair
To Somewhere, some land of who knows
What contours and flows.
The gardens all have pool and dike,
By every pool the same house stands,
In every house the same light shows,
And people all look alike
Covering their eyes with their hands.

In solchen Nächten werden die Sterbenden klar,
greifen sich leise ins wachsende Haar,
dessen Halme aus ihres Schädels Schwäche
in diesen langen Tagen treiben,
als wollten sie über der Oberfläche
des Todes bleiben.
Ihre Gebärde geht durch das Haus,
als wenn überall Spiegel hingen;
und sie geben—mit diesem Graben
in ihren Haaren—Kräfte aus,
die sie in Jahren gesammelt haben,
welche vergingen.

7

Such nights, the minds of the dying clear,
Their hands probe softly the growing hair
Whose stalks in those slow-moving days
Shoot forth and up from the skull's malaise
As if to stay above the sphere
of death.
That gesture runs through the house as though
Mirrors were hung on all the piers;
And by delving so
In that hair, they exhaust
Funds of strength gathered down the years
Now lost.

SCHLUSSTÜCK

Der Tod ist gross.
Wir sind die Seinen
Lachenden Munds.
Wenn wir uns mittem im Leben meinen,
Wagt er zu weinen
Mitten in uns.

CODA

Death is great.
We are in his keep
Laughing and whole.
When we feel deep
In life, he dares weep
Deep in our soul.

FRÜHER APOLLO

Wie manches Mal durch das noch unbelaubte
Gezweig ein Morgen durchsieht, der schon ganz
im Frühling ist: so ist in seinem Haupte
nichts, was verhindern könnte, dass der Glanz

Aller Gedichte uns fast tödlich träfe;
denn noch kein Schatten ist in seinem Schaun,
zu kühl für Lorbeer sind noch seine Schläfe,
und später erst wird aus den Augenbrau'n

hochstämmig sich der Rosengarten heben,
aus welchem Blätter, einzeln, ausgelöst
hintreiben werden auf des Mundes Beben,

der jetzt noch still ist, niegebraucht und blinkend
und nur mit seinem Lächeln etwas trinkend,
als würde ihm sein Singen eingeflößt.

EARLY APOLLO

Just as at times, through branches yet unclad,
A morning sends it gaze with more than a hint
Of spring: just so there is about his head
Nothing to hinder any poem's glint

From striking us with all but deadly thrill;
There is no shadow yet about his eyes,
Too cool for laurels is his temple still,
And only later from those brows will rise

The bank of roses, on their stems aloft,
Whence now and then a petal, wafting off,
Will drift on quavers of the mouth that yet

Is motionless, unused, and mutely shining—
The drinking-act with just its smile outlining,
As if its song were being spooned to it.

LIEBES-LIED

Wie soll ich meine Seele halten, daß
sie nicht an deine rührt? Wie soll ich sie
hinheben über dich zu andern Dingen?
Ach gerne möcht ich sie bei irgendwas
Verlorenem im Dunkel unterbringen
an einer fremden stillen Stelle, die
nicht weiterschwingt, wenn deine Tiefen schwingen.
Doch alles, was uns anrührt, dich und mich,
nimmt uns zusammen wie ein Bogenstrich,
der aus zwei Saiten *eine* Stimme zieht.
Auf welches Instrument sind wir gespannt?
Und welcher Geiger hat uns in der Hand?
O süßes Lied.

LOVE SONG

How am I to contain my spirit lest
It touch on yours? How lift it through a space
Higher than you to things environing?
Oh, I should gladly lay it by to rest
In darkness with some long-forgotten thing
At some outlandish unresounding place
Which won't re-echo your deep echoing.
But all that touches you and me comes so,
It takes us jointly like a stroking bow
That draws one voice from two strings by its tilt.
Upon what instrument then are we strung?
And by the hands of what musician wrung?
Ah, sweet the lilt.

GRABMAL EINES JUNGEN MÄDCHENS

Wir gedenkens noch. Das ist, als müßte
alles dieses einmal wieder sein.
Wie ein Baum an der Limonenküste
trugst du deine kleinen leichten Brüste
in das Rauschen seines Bluts hinein:

—jenes Gottes.
               Und es war der schlanke
Flüchtling, der verwöhnende der Fraun.
Süss und glühend, warm wie dein Gedanke,
überschattend deine frühe Flanke
und geneigt wie deine Augenbrau'n.

GRAVESTONE OF A YOUNG GIRL

Still we mind it. All that was before
Must be back one morning, it would seem.
Like a tree upon the citrus shore,
Your unweighing little breasts you bore
Deep into his blood's onrushing stream:

His of all the gods.
                         It was the slender
Fugitive, to women fondly tender;
Sweet and incandescent, like your mind,
Overshadowing your girlish loin
And inclining like your eyebrows' camber.

PIETÀ

So seh ich, Jesus, deine Füsse wieder,
die damals eines Jünglings Füsse waren,
da ich sie bang entkleidete und wusch;
wie standen sie verwirrt in meinen Haaren
und wie ein weisses Wild im Dornenbusch.

So seh ich deine niegeliebten Glieder
zum ersten Mal in dieser Liebesnacht.
Wir legten uns noch nie zusammen nieder,
und nun wird nur bewundert und gewacht.

Doch siehe, deine Hände sind zerrissen—:
Geliebter, nicht von mir, von meinen Bissen.
Dein Herz steht offen, und man kann hinein:
Das hätte dürfen nur mein Eingang sein.

Nun bist du müde, und dein müder Mund
Hat keine Lust zu meinem wehen Munde—.
O Jesus, Jesus, wann war unsre Stunde?
Wie gehn wir beide wunderlich zugrund.

PIETÀ

Thus, Jesus, do I see your feet again?
Those feet which last time were a slender lad's,
When timidly I bared and washed them here;
How they forlornly stood among my plaits
Like, in a thornbush caught, a milk-white deer.

So now I see your limbs, unfondled ever,
For the first time, at this our lover's tryst.
We never in our time lay down together;
Now to adore and watch is all there is.

But look, your hands are mangled at the center—:
What bites, belovèd—they were not my own.
Your heart is open, anyone's to enter:
That was to have been my door, mine alone.

Now you are weary, and your mouth too wry
To have a longing for my suffering lips—.
O Jesus, Jesus, whence came our eclipse?
How quirkily we perish, you and I.

DER TOD DES DICHTERS

Er lag. Sein aufgestelltes Antlitz war
bleich und verweigernd in den steilen Kissen,
seitdem die Welt und dieses von-ihr-Wissen,
von seinen Sinnen abgerissen,
zurückfiel an das teilnahmslose Jahr.

Die, so ihn leben sahen, wußten nicht,
wie sehr er Eines war mit allem diesen:
denn Dieses: diese Tiefen, diese Wiesen
und diese Wasser *waren* sein Gesicht.

O sein Gesicht war diese ganze Weite,
die jetzt noch zu ihm will und um ihn wirbt:
und seine Maske, die nun bang verstirbt,
ist zart und offen wie die Innenseite
von einer Frucht, die an der Luft verdirbt.

DEATH OF THE POET

He lies there; the upslanted face appears
Pale and denying in the pillow's skew,
Now that the outer world, and that he knew
Of it, torn off from sense and view,
Has fallen back to the indifferent years.

Those knowing him alive were unaware
He was so of a piece with all of this:
For these, the sunken lands, the meadows there,
These waters, up to then had *been* his face.

His face—oh yes—was all that far-and-wide
Which still is seeking out and wooing him;
While this, his mask, now growing sadly dim,
Lies tender and exposed like the inside
Of an aired fruit decaying at the rim.

GOTT IM MITTELALTER

Und sie hatten ihn in sich erspart,
und sie wollten, dass er sei und richte,
und sie hängten schließlich wie Gewichte
(zu verhindern seine Himmelfahrt)

an ihn ihrer großen Kathedralen
Last und Masse. Und er sollte nur
über seine grenzenlosen Zahlen
zeigend kreisen und wie eine Uhr

Zeichen geben ihrem Tun und Tagwerk.
Aber plötzlich kam er ganz in Gang,
und die Leute der entsetzten Stadt

ließen ihn, vor seiner Stimme bang,
weitergehn mit ausgehägtem Schlagwerk
und entflohn vor seinem Zifferblatt.

GOD IN THE MIDDLE AGES

They had saved Him up within themselves,
Wanting Him to be in place and govern,
Even settled their cathedrals' hovering
Mass and heft on Him like granite shelves,

Barring his ascension. He was free
Just to "tell" like clock-hands and revolve
Through his numbers' rank infinity
As a pointer, and—thus their resolve—

Furnish signals for their chores and times.
Of a sudden, though, His wheels were spinning,
And the people of the awestruck town

Fearfully imagining His dinning,
Kept him running with suspended chimes
And fled headlong from His dial's frown.

MORGUE

Da liegen sie bereit, als ob es gälte,
nachträglich eine Handlung zu erfinden,
die miteinander und mit dieser Kälte
sie zu versöhnen weiß und zu verbinden;

denn das ist alles noch wie ohne Schluß.
Was für ein Name hätte in den Taschen
sich finden sollen? An dem Überdruß
um ihren Mund hat man herumgewaschen;

er ging nicht ab; er wurde nur ganz rein.
Die Bärte stehen, noch ein wenig härter,
doch ordentlicher im Geschmack der Wärter,

nur um die Gaffenden nicht anzuwidern.
Die Augen haben hinter ihren Lidern
sich umgewandt und schauen jetzt hinein.

IN THE MORGUE

In readiness they lie there as if told
Belatedly to postulate an act
Which stood to reconcile them with this cold
And join them to each other in some pact;

For all of this does not seem final yet.
What sort of name had anyone expected
To find in what they wore? The queasy set
That made their mouths wry, someone had directed

To be scrubbed off—which only left them clean.
The whiskers now stand up a little harder,
Yet neater by the notions of the warder,

Less apt to make the gapers' gorges rise;
Behind the lids, the apples of their eyes
Have turned about, their target now within.

DER PANTHER

Im Jardin des Plantes, Paris

Sein Blick ist vom Vorübergehn der Stäbe
so müd geworden, daß er nichts mehr hält.
Ihm ist, als ob es tausend Stäbe gäbe
und hinter tausend Stäben keine Welt.

Der weiche Gang geschmeidig starker Schritte,
der sich im allerkleinsten Kreise dreht,
ist wie ein Tanz von Kraft um eine Mitte,
in der betäubt ein großer Wille steht.

Nur manchmal schiebt der Vorhang der Pupille
sich lautlos auf—. Dann geht ein Bild hinein,
geht durch der Glieder angespannte Stille—
und hört im Herzen auf zu sein.

THE PANTHER
Jardin des Plantes, Paris

His gaze has been so worn by the procession
Of bars that it no longer makes a bond.
Around, a thousand bars seem to be flashing,
And in their flashing show no world beyond.

The lissom steps which round out and re-enter
That tightest circuit of their turning drill
Are like a dance of strength about a center
Wherein there stands benumbed a mighty will.

Only from time to time the pupil's shutter
Will draw apart: an image enters then,
To travel through the tautened body's utter
Stillness—and in the heart to end.

By way of commentary on "The Panther," the translator's latest English version, presented above, is augmented by critical comparisons of earlier translations by others and himself; see p. 159.

DIE GAZELLE

Gazella Dorcas

Verzauberte: wie kann der Einklang zweier
erwählter Worte je den Reim erreichen,
der in dir kommt und geht, wie auf ein Zeichen.
Aus deiner Stirne steigen Laub und Leier,

und alles Deine geht schon im Vergleich
durch Liebeslieder, deren Worte, weich
wie Rosenblätter, dem, der nicht mehr liest,
sich auf die Augen legen, die er schließt:

um dich zu sehen: hingetragen, als
wäre mit Sprüngen jeder Lauf geladen
und schösse nur nicht ab, solang der Hals

das Haupt ins Horchen hält: wie wenn beim Baden
im Wald die Badende sich unterbricht:
den Waldsee im gewendeten Gesicht.

*This poem, one of the triumphs of Rilke's evocative art, is also remark-
able structurally for building a sonnet from two vastly asymmetric pieces
of syntax: a three-line rhetorical question, and a now subsiding, now resum-
ing, now catapulting, now telescoping answer in a single 11-line sentence.
This linguist, connoisseur of German Schachtelsätze (box-within-box sen-
tences, syntactic embedding), fondly recalls the famous example of a Ger-
man notice allegedly found on a post by a pond: "Der, der den, der den
Pfahl, auf dem geschrieben stand, 'Hier darf nichts ins Wasser geworfen
werden,' selbst ins Wasser geworfen hat, anzeigt, erhalt 50M Belohnung."
Translation à la Mark Twain: "He who him, who has the post on which it
said 'No throwing of objects into the water' itself into the water thrown,
reports, receives a 50M reward."*

Disengaging the long central sequence in our Gazelle poem from the

THE GAZELLE

Gazella Dorcas

Enchanted one: how can one harmonize
Two chosen words so as to reach the rhyme
Which comes and goes in you, as by a sign.
From out your forehead leaf and lyre arise,

All yours in metaphor already goes
Through songs of love whose phrases, soft as rose
Petals, descend upon the eyes of those
Who read no more because their eyelids close

That they may see you: carried forth as if
Each slim leg were a barrel charged with bounding,
Just kept from discharge while the neck is stiff

With hearkening: as when a bather, rounding
Upon a woodland noise, stops in surprise,
The forest pool still in her backturned eyes.

gear train of the verse, we get: "All that is yours is figuratively current
already in songs of love whose words, soft as rose petals, settle on the eyes
of him who no longer reads, as he closes them in order to see you."

This remote metaphor, seeping into the poem through a labyrinth of
dependent clauses, induces a pleasant vertigo, sharpened perhaps by the
suggestion that one closes rose-petal-strewn eyelids to open them to the
sight of a piece of living statuary in a stance of surpassing grace. And the
two closing tercets certainly wreak magic, one of the great glories of Rilke's
poetry. Notice, incidentally, the language cocking a snoot at the translator:
German Lauf serendipitously injects into the poem three relevant meanings
(out of the dozens associated with the morpheme): 1. a wild animal's leg;
2. the barrel of a rifle or gun, from the 'runnel' offered to the bullet; 3. the
action of running; course.

DER SCHWAN

Diese Mühsal, durch noch Ungetanes
schwer und wie gebunden hinzugehn,
gleicht dem ungeschaffnen Gange des Schwanes.

Und das Sterben, dieses Nichtmehrfassen
jenes Grunds, auf dem wir täglich stehn,
seinem ängstlichen Sich-Niederlassen—:

in die Wasser, die ihn sanft empfangen
und die sich, wie glücklich und vergangen,
unter ihm zurückziehn, Flut um Flut;
während er unendlich still und sicher
immer mündiger und königlicher
und gelassener zu ziehn geruht.

THE SWAN

This great toil: to go through things undone
Plodding as if tied by foot and hand,
Recalls the uncouth walking of the swan;

Death, the loss of grip upon the shelf
Whereon every day we used to stand,
Mimes the anxious launching of himself

On the floods where he is gently caught,
Which, as if now blessèdly at naught,
Float aside beneath him, ring by ring;
While he, infinitely sure and calm,
Ever more of age and free of qualm,
Deigns to fare upon them like a king.

DER DICHTER

Du entfernst dich von mir, du Stunde.
Wunden schlägt mir dein Flügelschlag.
Allein: was soll ich mit meinem Munde?
mit meiner Nacht? mit meinem Tag?

Ich habe keine Geliebte, kein Haus,
keine Stelle auf der ich lebe.
Alle Dinge, an die ich mich gebe,
werden reich und geben mich aus.

THE POET

Farther from me, o hour, you grow.
Your wingbeat wounds me upon its way.
What would I do with my lips, though?
With my night? With my day?

I have no beloved, no shelter,
No homestead at which to be.
All things I lavish my self on
Grow rich and lavish me.

DIE ERBLINDENDE

Sie saß so wie die anderen beim Tee.
Mir war zuerst, als ob sie ihre Tasse
ein wenig anders als die andern fasse.
Sie lächelte einmal. Es tat fast weh.

Und als man schließlich sich erhob und sprach,
und langsam, und wie es der Zufall brachte,
durch viele Zimmer ging (man sprach und lachte),
da sah ich sie. Sie ging den andern nach,

verhalten, so wie eine welche gleich
wird singen müssen, und vor vielen Leuten;
auf ihren hellen Augen, die sich freuten,
war Licht von aussen wie auf einem Teich.

Sie folgte langsam, und sie brauchte lang,
als wäre etwas noch nicht überstiegen;
und doch als ob nach einem Übergang,
sie nicht mehr gehen würde, sondern fliegen.

GOING BLIND

She sat at tea just like the others. First
I merely had a notion that this guest
Held up her cup not quite like all the rest.
And once she gave a smile. It almost hurt.

When they arose at last, with talk and laughter,
And ambled slowly and as chance dictated
Through many rooms, their voices animated,
I saw her seek the noise and follow after,

Held in like one who in a little bit
Would have to sing where many people listened;
Her lighted eyes, which spoke of gladness, glistened
With outward luster, as a pond is lit.

She followed slowly, and it took much trying,
As though some obstacle still barred her stride;
And yet as if she on the farther side
Might not be walking any more, but flying.

For another rendering of "Der Erblindende," and the present translator's detailed comments on it, see pp. 166–68.

TODESERFAHRUNG

Wir wissen nichts von diesem Hingehn, das
nicht mit uns teilt. Wir haben keinen Grund,
Bewunderung und Liebe oder Haß
dem Tod zu zeigen, den ein Maskenmund

tragischer Klage wunderlich entstellt.
Noch ist die Welt voll Rollen, die wir spielen,
Solang wir sorgen, ob wir auch gefielen,
spielt auch der Tod, obwohl er nicht gefällt.

Doch als du gingst, da brach in diese Bühne
ein Streifen Wirklichkeit durch jenen Spalt,
durch den du hingingst: Grün wirklicher Grüne,
wirklicher Sonnenschein, wirklicher Wald.

Wir spielen weiter. Bang und schwer Erlerntes
hersagend und Gebärden dann und wann
aufhebend; aber dein von uns entferntes,
aus unserm Stück entrücktes Dasein kann

uns manchmal überkommen, wie ein Wissen
von jener Wirklichkeit sich niedersenkend,
so daß wir eine Weile hingerissen
das Leben spielen, nicht an Beifall denkend.

INTIMATION OF REALITY

We have no clue to this departed state,
It does not share with us. We feel no task
To tender admiration, love, or hate
To Death, with whom the fretful stylized mask

Of tragedy so oddly misagrees.
The world is yet so full of parts we play.
While we still worry if we pleased that day,
Death also plays, although he does not please.

But when you left, there fell into the scene
A ray of realness through the very gap
By which you left us: greenness of true green,
Natural sunshine, forest real with sap.

We act, at times lay gestures by, recite
Things studied anxiously and hard by rote,
But of your being, now remote and quite
Translated from our daily play, a note

May sometimes sink upon us like a hint
Of that reality, and give us pause;
So that, swept up in it for a short stint,
We do real life, not thinking of applause.

For the background of this poem, whose title is literally translated "Experience of Death," see p. 169.

VOR DEM SOMMERREGEN

Auf einmal ist aus allem Grün im Park
man weiß nicht was, ein Etwas, fortgenommen;
man fühlt ihn näher an die Fenster kommen
und schweigsam sein. Inständig nur und stark

ertönt aus dem Gehölz der Regenpfeifer,
man denkt an einen Hieronymus:
so sehr steigt irgend Einsamkeit und Eifer
aus dieser einen Stimme, die der Guß

erhören wird. Des Saales Wände sind
mit ihren Bildern von uns fortgetreten,
als dürften sie nicht hören was wir sagen.

Es spiegeln die verblichenen Tapeten
das ungewisse Licht von Nachmittagen,
in denen man sich fürchtete als Kind.

BEFORE THE SUMMER RAIN

All of a sudden from the park's full green
Something, you can't say what, has been rescinded;
You feel it drawing closer to the windows
And growing silent. Fervently and keen

Resounds alone the rain-note of the plover,
Like some Jerome, so tensely from the brush
A sense of zeal and loneness arches over
Out of this single urgence, which the rush

Of rain will slake. The walls of the great hall,
Its pictures, have retreated like a hearer
Who must not overhear what we are saying;

The faded tapestries which line them mirror
Those afternoons of twilight mootly graying
In which we were afraid when we were small.

IM SAAL

Wie sind sie alle um uns, diese Herrn
in Kammerherrentrachten und Jabots,
wie eine Nacht um ihren Ordensstern
sich immer mehr verdunkelnd, rücksichtslos,
und diese Damen, zart, fragile, doch groß
von ihren Kleidern, eine Hand im Schooß,
klein wie ein Halsband für den Bologneser:
wie sind sie da um jeden: um den Leser,
um den Betrachter dieser Bibelots,
darunter manches ihnen noch gehört.

Sie lassen, voller Takt, uns ungestört
das Leben leben wie wir es begreifen
und wie sie's nicht verstehn. Sie wollten blühn,
und blühn ist schön sein; doch wir wollen reifen,
und das heißt dunkel sein und sich bemühn.

IN THE HALL

How they are all about, these gentlemen
In chamberlains' apparel, stocked and laced,
Like night around their order's star and gem
And growing ever darker, stony-faced,
And these, their ladies, fragile, wan, but propped
High by their bodice, one hand loosely dropped,
Small like its collar, on the toy King-Charles:
How they surround each one of these who stopped
To read and contemplate the objets d'art,
Of which some pieces still are theirs, not ours.

With exquisite decorum they allow us
A life of whose dimensions we seem sure
And which they cannot grasp. They were alive
To bloom, that is be fair; we, to mature,
That is to be of darkness and to strive.

LETZTER ABEND

Und Nacht und fernes Fahren; denn der Train
des ganzen Heeres zog am Park vorüber.
Er aber hob den Blick vom Clavecin
und spielte noch und sah zu ihr hinüber

beinah, wie man in einen Spiegel schaut:
so sehr erfüllt von seinen jungen Zügen
und wissend, wie sie seine Trauer trügen,
schön und verführender bei jedem Laut.

Doch plötzlich wars, als ob sich das verwische:
sie stand wie mühsam in der Fensternische
und hielt des Herzens drängendes Geklopf.

Sein Spiel gab nach. Von draußen wehte Frische.
Und seltsam fremd stand auf dem Spiegeltische
der schwarze Tschako mit dem Totenkopf.

LAST EVENING

Nighttime and distant rumbling; for the train
Of all the army passed the parkgate there.
He raised his eyes up from the clavecin
While playing still, and looked across to her

Almost as though into a looking-glass:
So wholly in his own young face absorbed
And knowing how it let his sadness pass,
More comely and seductive with each chord.

But of a sudden something blurred the view:
She faltered in her niche as if unable
To smother the insistent heartbeat's tones.

His play gave in. From outside coolness blew.
And, strangely alien, on the mirror table
Stood the black busby with the skull and bones.

SELBSTBILDNIS AUS DEM JAHRE 1906

Des alten lange adligen Geschlechtes
Feststehendes im Augenbogenbau.
Im Blicke noch der Kindheit Angst und Blau
und Demut da und dort, nicht eines Knechtes,
doch eines Dienenden und einer Frau.
Der Mund als Mund gemacht, groß und genau,
nicht überredend, aber ein Gerechtes
Aussagendes. Die Stirne ohne Schlechtes
und gern im Schatten stiller Niederschau.

Das, als Zusammenhang, erst nur geahnt;
noch nie im Leiden oder im Gelingen
zusammgefaßt zu dauerndem Durchdringen,
doch so, als wäre mit zerstreuten Dingen
von fern ein Ernstes, Wirkliches geplant.

*In the case of the "Self-Portrait," if we trust poets as translators of poetry,
we may hope for once to present, by way of an earlier rendering, not a
tattered derelict sharing with its model barely a rag, a bone, and a hank of
hair, but a fascinating poetic artifact which aspires to be not a translation
but an "imitation." It is found in Robert Lowell's well-known volume of
1958, an assembly of treatments of poetic texts from Homer to Pasternak
which he called "Imitations." Although it preserves a distinct kinship in
structure and reflection to Rilke's "Self-Portrait," this particular specimen
takes off from it into an efflorescence of detail, a lively elaboration of color
and statement that nowhere departs far, yet by the end makes the "imitation"
relate to the sober and introspective original somewhat like a supercharged
bantam to a brood-hen.*

SELF-PORTRAIT

The bone-build of the eyebrows has a mule's
or Pole's noble and narrow steadfastness.
A scared blue child is peering through the eyes,
and there's a kind of weakness, not a fool's,
yet womanish—the gaze of one who serves.
The mouth is just a mouth . . . untidy curves,
quite unpersuasive, yet it says its *yes*,
when forced to act. The forehead cannot frown,
and likes the shade of dumbly looking down.

SELF-PORTRAIT, 1906

The long-enduring, once ennobled clan's
Stability in how the browbones skew.
Gaze still imbued with childhood's fear and blue,
And meekness, yes, but not a hired man's,
A woman's or retainer's, willing due.
The mouth shaped as a mouth, wide-lipped and true,
Not to persuade but to give utterance
To just thought. Brow without offense,
Glad in the shade of quiet downward view.

This, as a whole, is still at most divined;
Never as yet in suffering or fruition
Combined to an enduring coalition,
But still, as if with scattered ammunition
A real and serious action were outlined.

A still life, *nature morte*—hardly a whole!
It has done nothing worked through or alive,
in spite of pain, in spite of comforting . . .
Out of this distant and disordered thing
something in earnest labors to unroll.

Why the "mule's or Pole's"? Why not the "donkey's or Boston Brahmin's"?
Because the line has to rhyme with "fool's" in the fourth line. Why does a
blue-eyed child become a blue baby? And what is one to make of "not a
fool's weakness, YET womanish"? Rilke's brow has "nothing poor (or bad or
mean) about it"; Lowell's "cannot frown," in order to furnish a rhyme for
"dumbly looking down." Lowell's "in spite of pain, in spite of comforting,"
on the other hand, argues not playful adornment or venial fudging but
gross ignorance of German—which Hannah Arendt, whose help he acknowl-
edges, evidently did not have a chance to remedy. The scattered features, the
German poet says, have "never yet been gathered together in suffering or
achieving to an enduring integration . . ."
  It is difficult to decide whether a pedestrian version having a kind of
prosy accuracy but no verve is worse or better than a Lowellesque "imitation"
—the result of a spirited gallop off-course by an Anglophone poet seated
firmly on the hobby-horse of his own selfish talent.

AUFERSTEHUNG

Der Graf vernimmt die Töne,
Er sieht einen lichten Riß;
Er weckt seine dreizehn Söhne
Im Erbbegräbnis.

Er grüßt seine beiden Frauen
Ehrerbietig von weit—;
Und alle voll Vertrauen
Stehn auf zur Ewigkeit

Und warten nur noch auf Erich
Und Ulriken Dorotheen,
Die sieben- und dreizehnjährig
Sechzehnhundertzehn
Verstorben sind in Flandern,
Um heute vor den andern
Unbeirrt herzugehn.

RESURRECTION

The Count hears the trumpet kean,
Sees the tomb spring a brilliant fault;
He wakens his sons—thirteen—
In the family vault.

He bows to both his wives
With distant ceremony;
All trustfully rise to new lives
In eternity,

(Just waiting for Godfrey then
And Mary Doreen,
Who, aged six and thirteen,
In Flemish soil were buried
In sixteen hundred and ten)

In order once again
To lead the procession, unharried.

DIE KURTISANE

Venedigs Sonne wird in meinem Haar
ein Gold bereiten: aller Alchemie
erlauchten Ausgang. Meine Brauen, die
den Brücken gleichen, siehst du sie

hinführen ob der lautlosen Gefahr
der Augen, die ein heimlicher Verkehr
an die Kanäle schließt, so daß das Meer
in ihnen steigt und fällt und wechselt. Wer

mich einmal sah, beneidet meinen Hund,
weil sich auf ihm oft in zerstreuter Pause
die Hand, die nie an keiner Glut verkohlt,

die unverwundbare, geschmückt, erholt—.
Und Knaben, Hoffnungen aus altem Hause,
gehn wie an Gift an meinem Mund zugrund.

THE COURTESAN

Venetian sun will in my hair devise
A kind of gold: all alchemy's last stroke
And sovereignty. My eyebrows, which evoke
Those bridges, do you see them draw a yoke

Above the soundless peril of the eyes,
Which by a sympathetic sorcery
Commune with the canals, so that the sea
Will crest and ebb in them and vary. He

Who saw me once will hold my dog in spite
Because on him in absent moments browses
My hand, which is by ardour never charred,

And rests at ease, inviolate, jewel-starred . . .
And boys of blood, the hopes of ancient houses,
Die of my lips as of a lethal blight.

RÖMISCHE FONTÄNE
Borghese

Zwei Becken, eins das andre übersteigend
aus einem alten runden Marmorrand,
und aus dem oberen Wasser leis sich neigend
zum Wasser, welches unten wartend stand,

dem leise redenden entgegenschweigend
und heimlich, gleichsam in der hohlen Hand,
ihm Himmel hinter Grün und Dunkel zeigend
wie einen unbekannten Gegenstand;

sich selber ruhig in der schönen Schale
verbreitend ohne Heimweh, Kreis aus Kreis,
nur manchmal träumerisch und tropfenweis

sich niederlassend an den Moosbehängen
zum letzten Spiegel, der sein Becken leis
von unten lächeln macht mit Übergängen.

Rilke's portrayal—in a single, serpentine, predicateless sentence twisted into a sonnet—of the interplay of water among three basins is breathtaking in its complexity and sophistication. It contrasts interestingly, not wholly to its advantage perhaps, with an earlier poem by a Swiss visitor to the same Roman fountain. About the middle of the century the gifted novelist and balladist Conrad Ferdinand Meyer left us the following short lyric:

DER RÖMISCHE BRUNNEN

Aufsteigt der Strahl, und fallend gießt
er voll der Marmorschale Rund,
die, sich verschleiernd, überfließt
in einer zweiten Schale Grund;
die zweite gibt—sie wird zu reich—
der dritten wallend ihre Flut,
und jede nimmt und gibt zugleich
und strömt und ruht.

ROMAN FOUNTAIN

Borghese

Two basins, one the other overclimbing
Out of an ancient rounded marble rim,
And quietly from upper ones inclining
To lower waters there awaiting them,

The softly talking one with silence rhyming,
And secretly, its hand cupped as it were,
Past green and dark high heavens for it miming,
A thing of which it had been unaware,

Serenely spreading through its lovely shell
Ring out of ring, without nostalgia,
But rarely, drop by dreamy droplet, lacing

Its seepage down a pendent fringe of algae
To the last mirror sheet, which wreathes its basin
From underneath in smiles of interfacing.

*The beguilingly simple, lilting litany of flow and fall derived by C. F. Meyer
from the same model as Rilke's may be sensed to some degree from this
rendering by the present commentator:*

The jet ascends and, falling, goes
to fill the marble basin's round,
which shrouds itself and overflows
into a second basin's ground;
the second gives—abounding soon—
it surging billow to the next,
and each both takes and spends its boon
and flows and rests.

DAS KARUSSELL

Jardin du Luxembourg

Mit einem Dach und seinem Schatten dreht
sich eine kleine Weile der Bestand
von bunten Pferden, alle aus dem Land,
das lange zögert, eh es untergeht.
Zwar manche sind an Wagen angespannt,
doch alle haben Mut in ihren Mienen;
ein böser roter Löwe geht mit ihnen
und dann und wann ein weißer Elefant.

Sogar ein Hirsch ist da ganz wie im Wald,
nur daß er einen Sattel trägt und drüber
ein kleines blaues Mädchen aufgeschnallt.

Und auf dem Löwen reitet weiß ein Junge
und hält sich mit der kleinen heißen Hand,
dieweil der Löwe Zähne zeigt und Zunge.

Und dann und wann ein weißer Elefant.

Und auf den Pferden kommen sie vorüber,
auch Mädchen, helle, diesem Pferdesprunge
fast schon entwachsen; mitten in dem Schwunge
schauen sie auf, irgendwohin, herüber—

Und dann und wann ein weißer Elefant.

Und das geht hin und eilt sich, daß es endet,
und kreist und dreht sich nur und hat kein Ziel.
Ein Rot, ein Grün, ein Grau vorbeigesendet,
ein kleines kaum begonnenes Profil.
Und manchesmal ein Lächeln, hergewendet,
ein seliges, das blendet und verschwendet
an dieses atemlose blinde Spiel.

MERRY-GO-ROUND

Jardin du Luxembourg

Beneath an awning and its shade revolving,
There passes every little while the stand
Of dappled horses, hailing from the land
Which lingers long before at last dissolving.
Some, to be sure, parade to harness bent,
But all display a mettlesome expression;
A fierce red lion rides in the procession,
And now and then a snow-white elephant.

You even have, as in the wood, a stag,
Though he is saddled too and bears along
A sky-blue little girl strapped to his back.

A boy in white is holding by a thong
Onto the lion with his small hot hand,
The lion meanwhile baring teeth and tongue.

And now and then a snow-white elephant.

And here they swing alongside on the horses,
Some girls all bright among them, who appear
Almost too old for this; and in mid courses
They lift their eyes to something over here—

And now and then a snow-white elephant.

All this goes by and hastens to its ending
And turns and circles, aimless in its run.
Some red, some green, some grey is borne along us,
A sketchy profile hardly yet begun—
From time to time a smile is turned upon us,
A smile that blinds with blitheness, overspending
Upon this gasping sightless round of fun . . .

DIE INSEL I

Nordsee

Die nächste Flut verwischt den Weg im Watt,
und alles wird auf allen Seiten gleich;
die kleine Insel draußen aber hat
die Augen zu; verwirrend kreist der Deich

um ihre Wohner, die in einen Schlaf
geboren werden, drin sie viele Welten
verwechseln schweigend; denn sie reden selten,
und jeder Satz ist wie ein Epitaph

für etwas Angeschwemmtes, Unbekanntes,
das unerklärt zu ihnen kommt und bleibt.
Und so ist alles, was ihr Blick beschreibt,

von Kindheit an: nicht auf sie Angewandtes,
zu Großes, Rücksichtsloses, Hergesandtes,
das ihre Einsamkeit noch übertreibt.

THE ISLAND I
North Sea

The tide will blur what path there was, so as
To make both sides, and all about, alike;
But far out there the little island has
Its eyes shut tight. Bewilderingly the dike

Encircles its inhabitants, all bred
Into a sleep where, silent, they confuse
Their many worlds; for speech they seldom use,
And every phrase is like a requiem read

For flotsam unencountered here before,
Arriving unexplained and cast ashore.
And such is everything their gaze addressed

From childhood up: things not applied to them,
Too large, too ruthless, sent into their ken,
By which their loneliness is further stressed.

DIE INSEL II

Nordsee

Als läge er in einem Kraterkreise
auf einem Mond: ist jeder Hof umdämmt,
und drin die Gärten sind auf gleiche Weise
gekleidet und wie Waisen gleich gekämmt

von jenem Sturm, der sie so rauh erzieht
und tagelang sie bange macht mit Toden.
Dann sitzt man in den Häusern drin und sieht
in schiefen Spiegeln, was auf den Kommoden

Seltsames steht. Und einer von den Söhnen
tritt abends vor die Tür und zieht ein Tönen
aus der Harmonika wie Weinen weich;

so hörte ers in einem fremden Hafen—.
Und draußen formt sich eines von den Schafen
ganz groß, fast drohend, auf dem Aussendeich.

THE ISLAND II

North Sea

Each house stands walled about behind the dike
As in the crater of a lunar ridge,
And all their garden plots are dressed alike
And combed alike as in an orphanage

By that which rears them with so rough a hand,
The Storm, and daunts them long with perishings.
Then people spend their time indoors and scan
By tilted mirrors what outlandish things

Stand on the chests of drawers. One of the sons
Steps just outside the door and draws some runs
From his hand-organ, gentle sobbing like,

As he has heard it at a far-off cape . . .
Outside, one of the sheep takes monstrous shape,
Almost of menace, on the outer dike.

DIE INSEL III
Nordsee

Nah ist nur Innres; alles andre fern.
Und dieses Innere gedrängt und täglich
mit allem überfüllt und ganz unsäglich.
Die Insel ist wie ein zu kleiner Stern,

welchen der Raum nicht merkt und stumm zerstört
in seinem unbewussten Furchtbarsein,
so daß er, unerhellt und überhört,
allein,

damit dies alles doch ein Ende nehme,
dunkel auf einer selbsterfundnen Bahn
versucht zu gehen, blindlings, nicht im Plan
der Wandelsterne, Sonnen und Systeme.

THE ISLAND III

North Sea

Only the inward is close; everything else is far;
And this inward is thronged with a daily duress,
Overcharged with it all, impossible to express.
The island is like too minute a star,

Which space has not perceived but mutely scored
With that unconscious dreadness of its own,
So that the star, unlighted and ignored,
Alone,

Just to enforce an end to this unease,
Invents an orbit for the one that missed him,
In darkness blundering, outside the system
Of coursing planets, suns, and galaxies.

ARCHAÏSCHER TORSO APOLLOS

Wir kannten nicht sein unerhörtes Haupt,
darin die Augenäpfel reiften. Aber
sein Torso glüht noch wie ein Kandelaber,
in dem sein Schauen, nur zurückgeschraubt,

sich hält und glänzt. Sonst könnte nicht der Bug
der Brust dich blenden, und im leisen Drehen
der Lenden könnte nicht ein Lächeln gehen
zu jener Mitte, die die Zeugung trug.

Sonst stünde dieser Stein entstellt und kurz
unter der Schultern durchsichtigem Sturz
und flimmerte nicht so wie Raubtierfelle;

und bräche nicht aus allen seinen Rändern
aus wie ein Stern: denn da ist keine Stelle,
die dich nicht sieht. Du mußt dein Leben ändern.

Käte Hamburger, in her Rilke: An Introduction *(1975), on the archetypical character of "Archaic Torso of Apollo" as an object poem (tr. W.A.):*

We are going to begin by choosing a few unmistakable object poems, which will enable us to demonstrate the Rilkean way of unleashing "innerness" from the surface . . . We shall start with one of the most famous poems, "Archaic Torso of Apollo," which introduces the second part of *Neue Gedichte*, for it brings out more clearly than any other what Rilke meant by treatment of a sculpture's surface. This treatment leaves the status of the archaic statue of Apollo in such a condition that the viewer experiences the torso only as the expression of a head of which we know nothing but that it must have been "unheard of." This insubstantial epithet, which merely evokes something vaguely immense, receives its semantic impregnation from the sememes of radiance and glitter used in describing the various parts of the body: glows, shines, dazzle, shimmer, shedding light like a star; all this in the subjunctive of unreal condition, which establishes much more suggestively than an indicative would have the improbability, the prodigy of this torso and, as it were, brings about the restoration of the lost head that must have been the cause of the inspirited body. The variously apportioned attributions of gleaming

ARCHAIC TORSO OF APOLLO

We have no inkling of the fabled head
Wherein the eyeballs ripened. Even so
His trunk still sends a candelabrum glow
By which his gaze, with just its wick set low,

Persists and gleams. Else could the torso's curve
Not so bedazzle you, nor with the shifting
Of loins could then a vagrant smile be drifting
Toward that center point, begetting's nerve.

Else would this boulder stand, defaced and squat,
Beneath the shoulders' lucent fall, and not
Ashimmer like the coat of some wild beast;

Nor would it then through every margin knife
Forth like a star: for there is not the least
Of parts but sees you. You must change your life.

and sparkle—are they set here as real properties of the marble which shines and reflects with light and shade? No—they are metaphors for the overwhelming, self-radiating expressiveness of this work of art, derived in its turn from the hypothetically "restored" unheard-of head. Moreover, in and through the poem's language the archaic artifact is brought into existence, and even the god himself whom it represents.

Left for us to consider are the much riddled-over and doubtless variously construable final phrases: "for there is no place that does not see you. You must change your life." They confirm, I believe, the fundamental attitude of this poet to what Is, represent the utmost intensification of the mood of his poem "Progress," with its lines "The things grow ever more akin to me / And ever more observed all images." We speak of utmost intensification because now, in the face of the unexampled liveness of this statue, mere inspection would no longer be the adequate and appropriate response. The need to be equal to this, to meet the claim this work of art makes on the viewer—"for there is no place that does not see you"—breeds the desire to turn into a different person oneself; in what way and in what direction remains open, unless one wishes to appoint the ever more intensively cultivated capacity for viewing itself as the task of a lifetime.

KRETISCHE ARTEMIS

Wind der Vorgebirge: war nicht ihre
Stirne wie ein lichter Gegenstand?
Glatter Gegenwind der leichten Tiere,
formtest du sie: ihr Gewand

bildend an die unbewußten Brüste
wie ein wechselvolles Vorgefühl?
Während sie, als ob sie alles wüßte,
auf das Fernste zu, geschürzt und kühl,

stürmte mit den Nymphen und den Hunden,
ihren Bogen probend, eingebunden
in den harten hohen Gurt;

manchmal nur aus fremden Siedelungen
angerufen und erzürnt bezwungen
von dem Schreien um Geburt.

The noted Rilke scholar, Käte Hamburger, in her 1975 monograph Rilke:
An Introduction, *makes the following interesting comments (tr. W.A.) on*
"Kretische Artemis":

> The unequivocal "thing" or "object" poems are not (as indicated ear-
> lier) all there is to *Neue Gedichte,* provided one wishes to describe ade-
> quately what Rilke's "thing" poetry comprises in this collection. Let us
> present a few more poems which are beyond the unequivocal and, just for
> that, characteristic in their own way.
>
> Looking at "Cretan Artemis," a "sculptural" poem identified as such
> by its title, we may note at the outset that the present—the natural
> tense, *praesens tabulare,* for object poetry—in this image poem is replaced
> by the past. This produces a peculiar effect. The figure is loosened from
> its statuesque presence or timelessness; it is set in motion, or rather seen

CRETAN ARTEMIS

Wind of headlands, say: was not her brow
Like some incandescent thing?
Did you, nimble beasts' sleek counter-sough,
Shape her outline, modelling

Fabric close against the unconscious breasts
Like a changeable presentiment?
Meanwhile she, as if omniscient,
Coolly, skirt tucked high, on boundless quests

Stormed off with her maidens and her hounds,
Trying out her bow, fast-bound
In her hard tall girth;

Rarely hailed from some outlandish shire
And defeated, to her ire,
By the scream for birth.

in motion: the tunic that clings to the body is seen as shaped by an imagined and addressed breeze; while the figure of the goddess herself, shown running, is transposed back into the erstwhile present of her myth, where she was goddess of both the hunt and women in labor. Just this is effected by the preterit, which indicates past and opens up myth and history behind the timeless presence of the sculpture. Yet while knowledge of the myth seems to lift the figure out of its sculptural existence, rouse it to life, and in the final stanza lead it beyond the merely visible, the boundary of the pictorial or object poem is not violated. A statue is described, and it is its exterior, its surface, which reveals its inwardness, its Artemis nature, and is interpreted by the poet—a procedure already followed by the young Rilke in his portrait of Lorenzo Medici.

LEDA

Als ihn der Gott in seiner Not betrat,
erschrak er fast, den Schwan so schön zu finden;
er ließ sich ganz verwirrt in ihm verschwinden.
Schon aber trug ihn sein Betrug zur Tat,

bevor er noch des unerprobten Seins
Gefühle prüfte. Und die Aufgetane
erkannte schon den Kommenden im Schwane
und wußte schon: er bat um Eins,

das sie, verwirrt in ihrem Widerstand,
nicht mehr verbergen konnte. Er kam nieder
und halsend durch die immer schwächre Hand

ließ sich der Gott in die Geliebte los.
Dann erst empfand er glücklich sein Gefieder
und wurde wirklich Schwan in ihrem Schooß.

LEDA

The god, when entering him in his great need,
Almost took fright to find the swan so comely,
And disappeared within him all but numbly.
His ruse, though, rushed him headlong into deed

Ere he could try the unproven covering
For how it felt. And Leda, all outspread,
Saw through the swan who came in godly stead
And knew already that he begged a thing

Which, baffled in her effort to withstand,
She could conceal no more. The god came down,
And snaking past the ever feebler hand,

Released himself into the lovely one.
Then only relished he his feather gown,
In her embrace becoming truly swan.

DER TOD DER GELIEBTEN

Er wußte nur vom Tod, was alle wissen:
daß er uns nimmt und in das Stumme stößt.
Als aber sie, nicht von ihm fortgerissen,
nein, leis aus seinen Augen ausgelöst,

hinüberglitt zu unbekannten Schatten,
und als er fühlte, daß sie drüben nun
wie einen Mond ihr Mädchenlächeln hatten
und ihre Weise wohlzutun:

da wurden ihm die Toten so bekannt,
als wäre er durch sie mit einem jeden
ganz nah verwandt; er ließ die andern reden

und glaubte nicht und nannte jenes Land
das gutgelegene, das immersüße—.
Und tastete es ab für ihre Füße.

This delicate mood poem comes to rest on a necessarily inconclusive note:
thankful acceptance, by a young man who had thought himself "bereaved,"
of the death of the beloved not as a wrenching separation from himself and
this world, but rather as a complaisant gliding away, and as his own convey-
ance, by loving imagination, to her new country, one forever enriched by her
"girl's smile, like a moon" and her "way of being of comfort." A comparison
with the more famous ORPHEUS. EURYDIKE. HERMES is inescapable. Had

DEATH OF THE BELOVED

He only knew of death what others know:
That we are seized and thrust beyond surmise.
But when she, never wrested from him, no,
But delicately eased out of his eyes,

Went gliding over there to shades unknown,
And when he sensed that yonder, after this,
Her girl's smile like a moon was theirs to own,
And her way of bestowing bliss:

Then grew he with the dead so close a bond
As though he were as near-of-kin as brothers
With each of them; he heard the talk of others

And disbelieved, and called the land beyond
The finely-situate, the ever-sweet—
And tested it all over for her feet.

Orpheus found it in his heart to call Hades the "finely situate," the "ever-sweet" for harboring Eurydice, instead of challenging nature and the gods for her release, he might have known the (however illusory) surcease of this young relict and preserved for Eurydice the (however wretched, to someone like Achilleus) oblivion that precluded suffering. But what would have happened to the pathos of the most powerful of the myths of loss?

EINE SIBYLLE

Einst, vor Zeiten, nannte man sie alt.
Doch sie blieb und kam dieselbe Straße
täglich. Und man änderte die Maße,
und man zählte sie wie einen Wald

nach Jahrhunderten. Sie aber stand
jeden Abend auf derselben Stelle,
schwarz wie eine alte Zitadelle,
hoch und hohl und ausgebrannt;

von den Worten, die sich unbewacht
wider ihren Willen in ihr mehrten,
immerfort umschrieen und umflogen,
während die schon wieder heimgekehrten
dunkel unter ihren Augenbogen
saßen, fertig für die Nacht.

A SIBYL

They had called her old in bygone ages.
But she stayed, and came by that same trail
Every day. And they revised the scale,
Counting her by centuries, as one gauges

Stands of virgin forest. She would rear
Every evening at the selfsame place,
Blackened like the hollow carapace
Of a burnt-out watchtower, gaunt and sere;

Shrieked at constantly and circled tight
By rogue words that spawned in her and roamed,
Pullulating there against her will;
While the ones which had already homed
Roosted somberly upon the sill
Of her cheekbones, ready for the night.

ADAM

Staunend steht er an der Kathedrale
steilem Aufstieg, nah der Fensterrose,
wie erschreckt von der Apotheose,
welche wuchs und ihn mit einem Male

niederstellte über die und die.
Und er ragt und freut sich seiner Dauer,
schlicht entschlossen; als der Ackerbauer,
der begann und der nicht wußte, wie

aus dem fertig-vollen Garten Eden
einen Ausweg in die neue Erde
finden. Gott war schwer zu überreden;

und er drohte ihm, statt zu gewähren,
immer wieder, daß er sterben werde.
Doch der Mensch bestand: sie wird gebären.

ADAM

Dazed, he stands at the cathedral's steep
Upsurge, where the window-rose is,
As if scared by the apotheosis
Which had grown and by a sudden leap

Placed him over many a so-and-so.
And he looms there, glad of his firm presence,
Artless his resolve, as is the peasant's
Who had made a start and did not know

How to find, from lush and finished Eden,
A descent into the virgin earth.
God took a tremendous deal of wheedling,

And, so far from granting, he would cry,
Over and again, that he would die.
But the man held out: she would give birth.

EVA

Einfach steht sie an der Kathedrale
großem Aufstieg, nah der Fensterrose,
mit dem Apfel in der Apfelpose,
schuldlos-schuldig ein für alle Male

an dem Wachsenden, das sie gebar,
seit sie aus dem Kreis der Ewigkeiten
liebend fortging, um sich durchzustreiten
durch die Erde, wie ein junges Jahr.

Ach, sie hätte gern in jenem Land
noch ein wenig weilen mögen, achtend
auf der Tiere Eintracht und Verstand.

Doch da sie den Mann entschlossen fand,
ging sie mit ihm, nach dem Tode trachtend,
und sie hatte Gott noch kaum gekannt.

EVE

Plain, she stands by the cathedral's tall
Exaltation near the window-rose,
Apple in the apple-proffering pose,
Guiltlessly to blame once and for all

For the growing life she founded here
Since for love she left the unison
Of eternities to struggle on
Through the soil as does the youthful year.

Not that she would not have liked to stay
Somewhat longer in that grove, attending
To the beasts' astute and peaceful way;

But she found the man's resolve was set,
And she sought with him the lethal ending,
Having barely known the Lord as yet.

DER BLINDE
Paris

Sieh, er geht und unterbricht die Stadt,
die nicht ist auf seiner dunkeln Stelle,
wie ein dunkler Sprung durch eine helle
Tasse geht. Und wie auf einem Blatt

ist auf ihm der Widerschein der Dinge
aufgemalt; er nimmt ihn nicht hinein.
Nur sein Fühlen rührt sich, so als finge
es die Welt in kleinen Wellen ein:

eine Stille, einen Widerstand—,
und dann scheint er wartend wen zu wählen:
hingegeben hebt er seine Hand,
festlich fast, wie um sich zu vermählen.

BLIND MAN

Paris

Watch him make lacunae in the town,
Which his wandering presence makes unseen,
Like a crack of blackness wavering down
Through a shining cup. As on a screen,

World reflected paints itself on him,
But is not admitted to his core.
Sensing only stirs as from a slim
Catch of world in ripples on his shore:

Now a light resistance, now a calm—
Then he pauses (seeming to decide
On some choice) and raptly lifts his arm,
Almost festively, as to his bride.

EINE WELKE

Leicht, wie nach ihrem Tode
trägt sie die Handschuh, das Tuch.
Ein Duft aus ihrer Kommode
verdrängte den lieben Geruch,

an dem sie sich früher erkannte.
Jetzt fragte sie lange nicht, wer
sie sei (: eine ferne Verwandte),
und geht in Gedanken umher

und sorgt für ein ängstliches Zimmer,
das sie ordnet und schont,
weil es vielleicht noch immer
dasselbe Mädchen bewohnt.

WILTED

She wears her gloves and shawls
Lightly, as if after death.
A scent from her chest of drawers
Has ousted the flesh's dear breath

That once was her self-sensation.
When last has she thought to ask
Who she is (: some distant relation)?
She wanders bemused, her task

To care for a timid chamber
Which she tidies with care,
Because who knows but the same girl
May still be living there.

SCHWARZE KATZE

Ein Gespenst ist noch wie eine Stelle,
dran dein Blick mit einem Klange stößt;
aber da an diesem schwarzen Felle
wird dein stärkstes Schauen aufgelöst:

wie ein Tobender, wenn er in vollster
Raserei in Schwarze stampft,
jählings am benehmenden Gepolster
einer Zelle aufhört und verdampft.

Alle Blicke, die sie jemals trafen,
scheint sie also an sich zu verhehlen,
um darüber drohend und verdrossen
zuzuschauern und damit zu schlafen.
Doch auf einmal kehrt sie, wie geweckt,
ihr Gesicht und mitten in das deine:
und da triffst du deinen Blick im geelen
Amber ihrer runden Augensteine
unerwartet wieder: eingeschlossen
wie ein ausgestorbenes Insekt.

BLACK CAT

A phantom, even, still presents a spot
On which your glance impinges with a stir;
But your most strenuous gazing comes to naught,
Dissolved against this coat of sable fur:

As one frenzied, at the height of madding
Rage stampeding into black,
Will abruptly at the baulky padding
Of the cell lose steam and stagger back.

All the glances ever aimed at her
She appears to hide about her fur,
Quivering over them, baneful and glum,
Even in her sleep a part of her.
Of a sudden, though, her eyes will come
Straight for yours, as if she'd just been woken:
In the amber of her eyestones then
You encounter your own gaze again,
Startlingly encapsuled like the token
Of a fly in prehistoric gum.

DIE SCHWESTERN

Sieh, wie sie dieselben Möglichkeiten
anders an sich tragen und verstehn,
so als sähe man verschiedene Zeiten
duch zwei gleiche Zimmer gehn.

Jede meint, die andere zu stützen,
während sie doch müde an ihr ruht;
und sie können nicht einander nützen,
denn sie legen Blut auf Blut,

wenn sie sich wie früher sanft berühren
und versuchen, die Allee entlang
sich geführt zu fühlen und zu führen:
ach, sie haben nicht denselben Gang.

THE SISTERS

Notice how each sister wears and mirrors
Like potentials in unequal modes,
It's as though you saw disjointed eras
Pass through two identical abodes.

Each imagines she supports the other,
Yet goes limp on her, if but she knew;
They can't be of use to one another:
Laying blood on blood is all they do . . .

They may fondle as in times preceding
And attempt, in walking down the lane,
To be feeling led as well as leading:
But alas—their gaits are not the same.

DIE LIEBENDE

Das ist mein Fenster. Eben
bin ich so sanft erwacht.
Ich dachte, ich würde schweben.
Bis wohin reicht mein Leben,
und wo beginnt die Nacht?

Ich könnte meinen, alles
wäre noch Ich ringsum;
durchsichtig wie eines Kristalles
Tiefe, verdunkelt, stumm.

Ich könnte auch noch die Sterne
fassen in mir; so groß
scheint mir mein Herz; so gerne
ließ es ihn wieder los

den ich vielleicht zu lieben,
vielleicht zu halten begann.
Fremd, wie niebeschrieben
sieht mich mein Schicksal an.

Was bin ich unter diese
Unendlichkeit gelegt,
duftend wie eine Wiese,
hin und her bewegt,

rufend zugleich und bange,
daß einer den Ruf vernimmt,
und zum Untergange
in einem Andern bestimmt.

GIRL IN LOVE

That's my window. This minute
So gently did I alight
From sleep—was still floating in it.
Where has my life its limit
And where begins the night?

I could fancy all things around me
Where nothing but I as yet;
Like a crystal's depth, profoundly
Mute, translucent, unlit.

I have space to spare inside me
For the stars, too: so full of room
Feels my heart; so lightly
Would it let go of him, whom

For all I know I have started
To love, it may be to hold.
Strange as if never charted
Stares my fortune untold.

Why is it I am bedded
Beneath this infinitude,
Fragrant like a meadow,
Hither and thither moved,

Calling out, yet fearing
Someone might hear the cry,
Destined to disappearing
Within another I.

DAS ROSEN-INNERE

Wo ist zu diesem Innen
ein Außen? Auf welches Weh
legt man solches Linnen?
Welche Himmel spiegeln sich drinnen
in dem Binnensee
dieser offenen Rosen,
dieser sorglosen, sieh:
wie sie lose im Losen
liegen, als könnte nie
eine zitternde Hand sie verschütten.
Sie können sich selber kaum
halten; viele ließen
sich überfüllen und fließen
über von Innenraum
in die Tage, die immer
voller und voller sich schließen,
bis der ganze Sommer ein Zimmer
wird, ein Zimmer in einem Traum.

CORE OF THE ROSE

Where is to this inner
An outer? On what ache
Do they lay such linen?
And what heavens are mirrored within it,
In the sheltered lake
Of these open roses,
Carefree ones; understand
How they loosely lie in the looseness
As if never a hand,
Trembling, might spill them.
They all but fail in dwelling
Firm in themselves, and many a rose
Let itself be overfilled; and welling
Over with inner space, these stream
Into the days that, swelling,
More and more wealth enclose,
Till all of summer grows
Into a room, a room in a dream.

DAMENBILDNIS AUS DEN ACHTZIGER JAHREN

Wartend stand sie an den schwergerafften
dunklen Atlasdraperien,
die ein Aufwand falscher Leidenschaften
über ihr zu ballen schien;

seit den noch so nahen Mädchenjahren
wie mit einer anderen vertauscht:
müde unter den getürmten Haaren,
in den Rüschenroben unerfahren
und von allen Falten wie belauscht

bei dem Heimweh und dem schwachen Planen,
wie das Leben weiter werden soll:
anders, wirklicher, wie in Romanen,
hingerissen und verhängnisvoll,—

daß man etwas erst in die Schatullen
legen düfte, um sich im Geruch
von Erinnerungen einzulullen;
daß man endlich in dem Tagebuch

einen Anfang fände, der nicht schon
unterm Schreiben sinnlos wird und Lüge,
und ein Blatt von einer Rose trüge
in dem schweren leeren Medaillon,

welches liegt auf jedem Atemzug.
Daß man einmal durch das Fenster winkte;
diese schlanke Hand, die neuberingte,
hätte dran für Monate genug.

YOUNG LADY, CA. 1880

She stood waiting by the darkly furled
Heavy silken drapings now in fashion,
Which an outlay of fictitious passion
Seemed to be ballooning over her;

Since her girlhood's end, so recent still,
She has felt her life was someone else's:
Smothered underneath her piled-up tresses,
Inexperienced with ruffled dresses,
Eavesdropped on from every pleat and frill

In her homesickness, her weak resolve
That her life must enter a new state,
Different, more real, more like a novel,
Taking her by storm, dispensing fate—

Only then might she lay by some trifle
Which could later lull her with that scent—
Memory; do what she has long meant:
Find at last an onset to her diary

Which the very act of writing down
Would not brand absurdity or pose,
And to wear a petal of a rose
In the heavy locket, empty now,

That bears down on every breath. Just once
To stand up here, waving through the window;
Why, this slender hand, the newly ringed one,
Would not need more sustenance for months.

PERSISCHES HELIOTROP

Es könnte sein, daß dir der Rose Lob
zu laut erscheint für deine Freundin: Nimm
das schön gestickte Kraut und überstimm
mit dringend flüsterndem Heliotrop

den Bülbül, der an ihren Lieblingsplätzen
sie schreiend preist und sie nicht kennt.
Denn sieh: wie süße Worte nachts in Sätzen
beisammenstehn ganz dicht, durch nichts getrennt,
aus der Vokale wachem Violett
hindüftend durch das stille Himmelbett—:

so schließen sich vor dem gesteppten Laube
deutliche Sterne zu der seidnen Traube
und mischen, daß sie fast davon verschwimmt,
die Stille mit Vanille und mit Zimt.

PERSIAN HELIOTROPE

Perhaps you think the rose too loud a choice
Of praise for your belovèd: you may hope
For this fine-broidered foliage to outvoice
With urgent whisper of the heliotrope

The nightingale who in her dear haunts raises
Too shrill a eulogy from ignorance.
For see: as of a night sweet words in phrases
Stand tightly ranged without a severance,
And waft their vowels' wakeful violet scent
At large along the silent firmament—:

Thus merge before the quilted leafy musters
Emphatic asterisks to silken clusters
And charge (so as to leave it almost wan)
The hush with orchid scent and cinnamon.

DIE ENTFÜHRUNG

Oft war sie als Kind ihren Dienerinnen
entwichen, um die Nacht und den Wind
(weil sie drinnen so anders sind)
draußen zu sehn an ihrem Beginnen;

doch keine Sturmnacht hatte gewiß
den riesigen Park so in Stücke gerissen,
wie ihn jetzt ihr Gewissen zerriß,

da er sie nahm von der seidenen Leiter
und sie weitertrug, weiter, weiter . . . :

bis der Wagen alles war.

Und sie roch ihn, den schwarzen Wagen,
um den verhalten das Jagen stand
und die Gefahr.
Und sie fand ihn mit Kaltem ausgeschlagen;
und das Schwarze und Kalte war auch in ihr.
Sie kroch in ihren Mantelkragen
und befühlte ihr Haar, als bliebe es hier,
und hörte fremd einen Fremden sagen:
Ichbinbeidir.

ELOPEMENT

As a child she had escaped before
From her maids, to see the night and storm
(Since they are so different at home)
At their doings in the great outdoor;

Surely, though, no gale at night could shred
That great park as now her conscience did

When he bore her off the silken rung
And along, and on, and still along . . . .

Till nothing but the coach was there.

And she caught the smell of the black coach,
All about which, reined-in still,
Pursuit and peril were.
And she found it lined with something chill,
And the black and chill were in her too.
She shrank down into her collar fur
And felt her hair as if it was to stay;
And herself a stranger, heard a stranger say:
Iamwithyou.

ROSA HORTENSIE

Wer nahm das Rosa an? Wer wußte auch,
daß es sich sammelte in diesen Dolden?
Wie Dinge unter Gold, die sich entgolden,
entröten sie sich sanft, wie im Gebrauch.

Daß sie für solches Rosa nichts verlangen,
bleibt es für sie und lächelt aus der Luft?
Sind Engel da, es zärtlich zu empfangen,
wenn es vergeht, großmütig wie ein Duft?

Oder vielleicht auch geben sie es preis,
damit es nie erführe vom Verblühn.
Doch unter diesem Rosa hat ein Grün
gehorcht, das jetzt verwelkt und alles weiß.

PINK HYDRANGEA

Who thought such pink could be? Who knew it there
Accumulating in each blushing cluster?
Like gilded things which by and by unluster
They gently grow unred as if from wear.

That one should give such rosiness out free!
Does it stay theirs still, smiling where it went?
Are angels there to take it tenderly
As it surrenders, generous like a scent?

Or, it may be, they only let it go
That it might never learn of overblowing.
Beneath this pink there lurked a greenness, though,
Which listened and now fades away, all knowing.

AUS EINEM FRÜHLING

(Paris)

O alle diese Toten des April,
Der Fuhren Schwärze, die sie weiterbringen
Durch das erregte, übertriebene Licht:
Als lehnte sich noch einmal das Gewicht
Gegen zuviel Leichtwerden in den Dingen
Mürrischer auf . . . Da aber gehen schon,
Die gestern noch die Kinderschürzen hatten,
Erstaunt erwachsen zur Konfirmation;
Ihr Weiß ist eifrig wie vor Gottes Thron
Und mildert sich im ersten Ulmenschatten.

SPRING FRAGMENT

(Paris)

Oh all these dead of April,
The blackness of the carts that bring
Them on through roused exaggerated light:
As though all weight had tried its last to spite
The over-buoyancy of reborn things
With added rancor . . . See them dressed and filed,
Those now to be confirmed, each still half child,
Fresh out of aprons, startled to be grown.
Their white is zealous as before God's throne
Until the elms' first shadow makes it mild.

Immer wieder, ob wir der Liebe Landschaft auch kennen
und den kleinen Kirchhof mit seinen klagenden Namen
und die furchtbar verschweigende Schlucht, in welcher
  die andern
enden: immer wieder gehn wir zu zweien hinaus
unter die alten Bäume, lagern uns immer wieder
zwischen die Blumen, gegenüber dem Himmel.

Over again, however well we know
Love's landscape and the tiny graveyard's lament of
    names,
And the dread ravine of silence where others
Come to an end: over again, two of us go
Under the ancient trees, over again we lie
Among the flowers, facing the sky.

Schon kehrt der Saft aus jener Allgemeinheit,
die dunkel in den Wurzeln sich erneut,
zurück ans Licht und speist die grüne Reinheit,
die unter Rinden noch die Winde scheut.

Die Innenseite der Natur belebt sich,
verheimlichend ein neues Freuet euch;
und eines ganzen Jahres Jugend hebt sich,
unkenntlich noch, in starrende Gesträuch.

Des alten Nußbaums rühmliche Gestaltung
füllt sich mit Zukunft, außen grau und kühl;
doch junges Buschwerk zittert vor Verhaltung
unter der kleinen Vögel Vorgefühl.

By now the sap returns from the routineness
That redistills itself in rooted dark
Back to the light, and feeds the limpid greenness
Still shying from the wind beneath the bark.

All nature stirs inside with living essence
Still reining back a new Laetate's rush;
And an entire twelvemonth's adolescence,
Disguised as yet, ascends the bristling brush.

The ancient nut-tree's stately figuration
Fills up with future, cool outside and bare;
But sprouting hedgerows shake with pent elation
At little birds' forefeeling, which they share.

SONETTE AN ORPHEUS, II, 3

Spiegel: noch nie hat man wissend beschrieben,
was ihr in euerem Wesen seid.
Ihr, wie mit lauter Löchern von Sieben
erfüllten Zwischenräume der Zeit.

Ihr, noch des leeren Saales Verschwender—,
wenn es dämmert, wie Wälder weit . . .
Und der Lüster geht wie ein Sechzehn-Ender
durch eure Unbetretbarkeit.

Manchmal seid ihr voll Malerei.
Einige scheinen *in* euch gegangen—,
andere schicktet ihr scheu vorbei.

Aber die Schönste wird bleiben, bis
drüben in ihre enthaltenen Wangen
eindrang der klare, gelöste Narziss.

SONNETS TO ORPHEUS, II, 3

Mirrors: to this day no one gives
True word of your essence as mime;
You, interstices of time
Charged as with holes of sieves.

Wastrels even of blank domains
Farflung at dusk like a sylvan crag . . .
And the chandelier stalks your forbidden planes
Like a sixteen-point stag.

At times you swarm with a painted cast.
Some seem to vanish within.
Some you have warily ordered past.

But the loveliest will stay until
Narcissus invades her averted chin
From beyond with his limpid rill.

SONETTE AN ORPHEUS, II, 4

O dieses ist das Tier, das es nicht gibt.
Sie wußtens nicht und habens jeden Falls
—sein Wandeln. seine Haltung, seinen Hals,
bis in des stillen Blickes Licht—geliebt.

Zwar *war* es nicht. Doch weil sie's liebten, ward
ein reines Tier. Sie ließen immer Raum.
Und in dem Raume, klar und ausgespart,
erhob es leicht sein Haupt und brauchte kaum

zu sein. Sie nährten es mit keinem Korn,
nur immer mit der Möglichkeit, es sei.
Und die gab solche Stärke an das Tier,

dass es aus sich ein Stirnhorn trieb. Ein Horn.
Zu einer Jungfrau kam es weiß herbei—
und war im Silber-Spiegel und in ihr.

SONNETS TO ORPHEUS, II, 4

Behold, this is the beast that never was.
They, unaware, loved it in any case,
Loved all—its neck, its stance, its ambling pace,
Down to the light of its calm gaze. Because

They loved it though it wasn't, there was bred
The purest creature. They allowed it space.
And in that negative and abstract place
It lightly raised its head and hardly had

To be. They did not feed it barley-corn,
Just the contingency it might exist;
And this imparted to it such a spur

It drove a sprout from out its brow—a horn—
And gliding whitely to a virgin's wrist,
Grew patent in her mirror and in her.

Rilke to Tsvetaeva,
Tsvetaeva to Rilke

*Rilke's remarkable elegy to Marina Tsvetaeva stands here
for the entire form class, or poetic order, of Rilkean unrhymed
elegies in irregular disticha, which are not represented else-
where in this collection. Because of Marina Tsvetaeva's lofty
rank as a poet and the instant rapport sought and reached by
the two epistolary virtuosos (she was bilingual in Russian
and German and intimately familiar with Rilke's work, he
still retained his* Schwarm *for Russia), the present author
thought it appropriate to offer not only Rilke's elegy but, as a
suitable epitaph to their correspondence, Tsvetaeva's death-
defying lyrical apostrophe to Rilke, which she completed
several weeks after his death on December 29 and called
"A New Year's" (greeting? elegy? requiem?—in any case a
message exclusively for his ears and memory). This corre-
spondence was translated into English by the present trans-
lator and published as part of* Pasternak, Tsvetaeva, Rilke:
Letters, Summer 1926, Harcourt Brace Jovanovich, 1985.*

*It seems particularly important at this late juncture to
call attention to the brief but luxuriant efflorescence which
Tsvetaeva seems to have brought to the moribund Rilke's
last summer, even though their plans to meet never materi-
alized. It seems fitting in part because the Rainer-Marina
relationship was absolutely the only one in his life in which
his mind and another of equal rank confronted, recognized,
and electrified each other; and because a student of Rilke
will look in vain for even the name of Tsvetaeva in all but
one of the plethora of monographs and biographies hitherto
devoted to Rilke in German and English.*

ELEGIE

an Marina Zwetajewa-Efron

O die Verluste ins All, Marina, die stürzenden Sterne!
Wir vermehren es nicht, wohin wir uns werfen, zu
  welchem
Sterne hinzu! Im Ganzen ist immer schon alles gezählt.
So auch, wer fällt, vermindert die heilige Zahl nicht.
Jeder verzichtende Sturz stürzt in den Ursprung und
  heilt.
Wäre denn alles ein Spiel, Wechsel des Gleichen,
  Verschiebung,
nirgends ein Name und kaum irgendwo heimisch
  Gewinn?
Wellen, Marina, wir Meer! Tiefen, Marina, wir Himmel.
Erde, Marina, wir Erde, wir tausendmal Frühling, wie
  Lerchen,
die ein ausbrechendes Lied in die Unsichtbarkeit wirft.
Wir beginnens als Jubel, schon übertrifft es uns völlig;
plötzlich, unser Gewicht dreht zur Klage abwärts den
  Sang.
Aber auch so: Klage? Wäre sie nicht: jüngerer Jubel nach
  unten.
Auch die unteren Götter wollen gelobt sein, Marina.
So unschuldig sind Götter, sie warten auf Lob wie die
  Schüler.
Loben, du Liebe, laß uns verschwenden mit Lob.
Nichts gehört uns. Wir legen ein wenig die Hand um die
  Hälse
ungebrochener Blumen. Ich sah es am Nil in
  Kôm-Ombo.
So Marina, die Spende, selber verzichtend, opfern die
  Könige.
Wie die Engel gehen und die Türen bezeichnen jener zu
  Rettenden,
also rühren wir dieses und dies, scheinbar Zärtliche an.
Ach wie weit schon Entrückte, ach, wie Zerstreute,
  Marina,
auch noch beim innigsten Vorwand. Zeichengeber, sonst
  nichts.

ELEGY FOR MARINA TSVETAEVA

9 June 1926

Oh, those losses to space, Marina, the plummeting
stars!
We don't eke them out, wherever we rush to accrue
To which star! In the sum, all has long since been
forereckoned;
Nor does the falling star diminish the sanctified
number.
Every resigning plunge, flung to the origin, heals.

Might it then all be a game, permuting of equals, a
shifting,
Nowhere a name, and scarce anywhere domiciled gain?
Swells, Marina? we ocean, depths, Marina? we sky!
Earth, Marina? we Earth, we thousandfold spring, we
larks
Whom an eruption of song flings past the borders of
sight.
We commence it triumphant: already it wholly excels
us.
All of a sudden our weight bends the song down to
lament.
Still: might lament not be a childlike downturned
exulting?
Even the nethern gods would fain be exalted, Marina.
For so artless are gods, waiting like pupils for praise.

Praise, my cherished one, let us be lavish with praise.
Nothing is ours. A moment our hand may circle the
throat
Of unplucked flowers. On the Nile, at Kôm-Ombo, I saw
it:
Thus, Marina, sacrifice kings, themselves renouncing
the vow-gift.
As the angels go marking the doors of those to be saved,
Thus we touch upon this and then that, apparently
tender.
Oh, how far translated by now, how scattered, Marina,
Are we even at heartmost pretext. Signal-wavers, no
more.

Dieses leise Geschäft, wo es der Unsrigen einer
nicht mehr erträgt und sich zum Zugriff entschließt,
rächt sich und tötet. Denn daß es tödliche Macht hat,
merkten wir alle an seiner Verhaltung und Zartheit
und an der seltsamen Kraft, die uns aus Lebenden zu
Überlebenden macht. Nicht-Sein. Weißt du's, wie oft
trug uns ein blinder Befehl durch den eisigen Vorraum
neuer Geburt . . . Trug: uns? Einen Körper aus Augen
unter zahllosen Lidern sich weigernd. Trug das in uns
niedergeworfene Herz eines ganzen Geschlechts. An ein
   Zugvogelziel
trug er die Gruppe, das Bild unserer schwebenden
   Wandlung.
Liebende dürften, Marina, dürfen soviel nicht
von dem Untergang wissen. Müssen wie neu sein.
Erst ihr Grab ist alt, erst ihr Grab besinnt sich,
   verdunkelt   .
unter dem schluchzenden Baum, besinnt sich auf Jeher.
Erst ihr Grab bricht ein; sie selber sind biegsam wie
   Ruten;
was übermäßig sie biegt, ründet sie reichlich zum Kranz.
Wie sie verwehen im Maiwind! Von der Mitte des
   Immer,
drin du atmest und ahnst, schließt sie der Augenblick
   aus.
(O wie begreif ich dich, weibliche Blüte am gleichen
unvergänglichen Strauch. Wie streu ich mich stark n die
   Nachtluft,
die dich nächstens bestreift.) Frühe erlernten die Götter
Hälften zu heucheln. Wir in das Kreisen bezogen
füllten zum Ganzen uns an wie die Scheibe des Monds.
Auch in abnehmender Frist, auch in den Wochen der
   Wendung
niemand verhülfe uns je wieder zum Vollsein, als der
einsame eigene Gang über der schlaflosen Landschaft.

R.

(9. Juni 1926)

This most reticent thing—should one of the likes of us,
Able to bear it no more, make up his mind and snatch—

Takes its revenge and kills. For that it has death-dealing
    power
Was made clear to us all by its indrawn and delicate way,
and by that singular force that turns us from being alive
Into survivors. Not being: remember how often
Some unseeing decree would bear us through the chill
    forecourt
Of a rebirth. . . . Bear. . . . us? Bear a body of eyes
Balking beneath uncountable lids. Bear the heart in us,
The flung-down heart of a whole generation. Bear the
    group
To a goal-mark of migrant birds, the trope of our wafting
    mutation.

Those who love, Marina, they ought not, they must not
Know so much of extinction. Must be as new.
Old is at most their grave, only their grave remembers,
Dimmed by the tearful tree, the onset of time.
Only their grave caves in, themselves are supple as
    withes;
What might bend them too far, rounds them to opulent
    wreath.
How they disperse in the wind of May! From the middle
    of Always,
Where you breathe and bode, the moment excludes
    them.
(Oh, how I sense you, she-blossom grown on the same
Unperishing stock; how strongly I strew myself to the
    night air
Soon to waft over you.) The gods learned early
To simulate halves. But we, involved in the circling,
Filled ourselves out to be wholes like the moon disc.
Not in a waning phase, nor yet in the weeks of a turning,
Would there be man or thing to help us to fulness again
Save for our own lone walk over the sleepless land.

A NEW YEAR'S[1]

Happy New Year—new world—new home—new roof!
First good wishes to your new abode
(Piously mistermed a welling, lush one[2]—
Belly mush), a place of roar and rushing,
Like a Cavern of the Winds, forsaken.
Your first letter from your newly vacant
Country, where, alone, I eat my heart out,
While to you it is by now a part of
Some star. . . . By the rules of rear-guard battle
Your beloved becomes a never-was, past's chattel,
Where before she was out-of-this-world.
Shall I tell you of . . . yours? How I heard?
Earth shook not below nor avalanche aloft, this
Man came in—just anyone—(the one I love is
You). "A grave event, indeed, of tragic moment;
Marked by *Novosti* and *Dni*[3]. . . You'll comment?"
"Where did . . . ?" "In the Alps." (Spruce fronds in
   window;
Bed sheet.) "You don't see the press, I think? Oh,
For your piece, then . . ." "No." "But . . ." "Once for all."
(Loud:) "Too hard for me." (Inside: I? sell out Christ?)
"At that health resort." (Your rented paradise.)
"When?" "Last night; the day before . . . I don't recall. . . .
Coming to the Alcazar?" "I can't.
(Loud:) My family." (Play Judas? That I shan't.)

Happy Year Ahead (as of tomorrow's nearing)!—
Want to know what *I* did, right after hearing . . . ?
Tsk . . . that came out wrong. My fault of old.
Keeping life and death in quotes, tales told
Consciously by way of idle chatter.
Nothing of my doing, yet some matter
Came to pass that worked without a shadow

---

1. The noun one expects to follow this adjectival phrase, *poslaniye* (message) or *stikhotvoreniye* (poem), is not supplied.
2. A disdainful allusion to the Church Slavic burial service, which has the priest chant solace to the mourners: "His/her soul now reposes at the place of fruitfulness, the site of abundance." Tsvetaeva maliciously echoes the phrase with a rhyming one that evokes a complacent, jelly-bellied bourgeoisie.
3. Émigré Russian newspapers.

Or an echo!
         Now—how did you travel?
How was torn—but not to pieces—your
Heart? As tough on Orlov pacers whom
Eagles could not pass (you said!)[4] your breath of
Life was sucked away—or was it better,
Gentler? Heights and depths he pays no heed
Who rides truly Russian eagle steeds.
We have ties of blood to the nether world
While on this one. What a deft desertion!
I pronounce both "life" and "death" with a cautious
Smile—and you will touch it with your own!
I enounce both "life" and "death" with a starred
Footnote (oh, the night I wake for here:
Leaving this cerebral hemisphere
For a starry one!).
           Dear friend, please don't forget
What I tell you now: if Russian letters
And not German tumbled from my pen,
This is not to signal that by then
Nothing mattered, dead man's (beggar's) lot
Being to eat what comes, unblinking—but rather that
Ours, the nether world, at age thirteen I learned in
Novodevichye,[5] was omni-, not a-lingual.

Here I ask, then, not without dismay:
Do you ask no longer how to say
"Nest" in Russian? Well, the only rhyme on *gnёzda*
(Covering all kinds of nests) is *zvёzdy*.

I digress? But when the very idea
Of digressing from you can't appear!
Every impulse, each *Du Lieber* thought
Leads inside you—and what sense is wrought
(German be more kin to me than Russian,

---

4. Meaning race horses from Count Orlov's famous stables. His name is the same as, and derived from, the possessive adjective of *oryol* (eagle). Evidently Rilke had hit upon this artless pun.

5. The convent school Tsvetaeva attended.

Next to angel tongues) asserts that room
Is not where you're not, save in the tomb.
All that it was not, and all it was—
"Can it be that no one feels . . . a real . . . ?[6]
What's the place like, Rainer? How do you feel?
Positively, absolutely first
Eye encounter of the universe
(And of course, subsumed within the latter,
Of the poet) and the last with the planet,
Granted you once fully, and never afresh,
Not of bard and barrow, spirit and flesh
(Which to sever would offend the two),
But of you with you, you with the very you,
And—no favors for the seed of Zeus—
Not of Castor-you or Pollux-you,
You-marmoreal with you-who-burgeon,
Is this parting or meeting—but a converging
Eye to eye: both meeting and departing
First of kind.
                    How you surveyed then, starting
With your own hand (trace of inkstain on it)
From you ump-(how much?)-teen-mile-high summit
Or unending, for unstarting, height
Poised above the crystal dish of light,
Mediterranean and other silver.
All as it was not, all as it will be
With me, too, beyond the suburb's brow.
All as it was not, and all as it is now,
(Like to one on leave for an out-of-phase
Extra week!)—where else is there to gaze,
Elbow propped upon your box-seat rail,
From *this* world if not at *that* one; from *that* same
Where but at the long-suffering *this*.
Bellevue is where I live. A little place
Made of nests and branches. Quoting the guide:
"Bellevue. Stronghold commanding a splendid sight

6. Rilke's voice interrupts Tsvetaeva with a simple earthly plaint: "Isn't any-
body (missing) me at all?" She answers, in gently teasing irony, with a picture-
postcard inquiry.

Of all Paris; seat of the Gauls' Chimera . . ."
Over Paris—that's the nearer—but there's one farther;
Elbows propped upon the red plush margin,
How absurd it must to you appear,
Or must *they* to me, from those boundless spheres
These our Bellevues and Belvederes!

Rushing this and that way. Personal, urgent things.
New Year's almost here. What for, with whom to clink
Toasts across the board? What in? A cotton flake
For foam. Why? So it's striking twelve: And where's my
    stake
In this, what would I do at a New Year's shindy,
"Rainer's dead" a scanding phrase within me;
If *you* could, an eye like yours, just set,
Then life is not life and death not death.
This means (darkly now, when we meet I'll learn it)
That there's neither life nor death, but a third thing,
Which is new. For its sake ('27's straw
Spread for parting '26's withdrawal⁷—
What high joy to end and start with you!)
Should I raise my glass, then, to your glass
'Way across a board the eye can't pass,
Toasting this? No—not that tavern chime:
I to *you*, whose fusion yields the rhyme,
That third thing.
                        My glance across the table
Finds your cross. How many out-town places,
How much out-town space! To whom else flowers,
Waving, a bush? Those places peculiarly ours,
No one else's! Each sheaf,every single leaf!
Spots which are just yours-with-me (yours-with-
    yourself's).
(Need I say I'd even go to a Party bash
If with you?— So many places! And months—a rash!
Think in weeks! And faubourgs in a squall,

7. An allusion to the custom of spreading straw on the roadway outside a
dying man's house to muffle the traffic noise.

Bare of people! Mornings! And what all
Nightingales have not even started, surely!

So cooped up, my sight must function poorly;
You, up where you are, must clearly see:
Nothing ever came of you and me,
Such a pure and simple nothing-on-earth,
Tailor-made to just our size and girth,
That there was no need for altering.
Nothing but—look for no offbeat thing
(He who straggles off the beat is wrong!),
But for something that had (which? how long?)
Joined some harmony!
                        The eternal song:
Nothing, in some trait of it, is something,
Anything—if only from afar, a shade's
Shadow! What though it's that hour, that day,
That house—even the doomed, to scaffold driven,
That—that mouth—by memory are given!
Or did they dispose too shrewdly here?
Out of all of *that*, the nether *world* alone
Did we own, as we ourselves are mere
Glints of self, who for all *this*, took all *that* world!

Here's to that least built-up subdivision,
To your new place, Rainer, your new world!
To cognition's utmost margin hurled,
On new hearing, Rainer, your new vision!

All to you was irksome,
Friend and passion, too.
Here's to new sound, Echo!
Sound, to echo new!

Wondering, on the school bench, times past counting:
What would rivers there be like? And mountains?
Are views finer—free of tourist blight?
Eden's hilly, Rainer, am I right?
Thund'rous? Not for widows' bland pretensions—
Eden II, above the first's dimension?

Eden—terraced? Take the Tatra chain:
Eden *must* be amphitatra-shaped,
Yes! (On someone is the curtain drawn. . . .)
Rainer, I was right, no? God's a *growing*
Baobab tree? not only Roi Soleil.
Not just one God? Over Him holds sway
Another?
How is writing at your spa?
You and verse are *there*, of course: you *are*
Verse! Is writing hard in the other land?
With no desk for elbow, brow for hand,
Cheek for palm
Please write, by the usual code!
Happy in a novel rhyming mode?
For, interpreting the word aright,
What is Rhyme but (here a swarming flight of
New rhymes settle) Death?
Gone: mastered his tongue.
Whole arrays of senses, assonances rung,
New!
Here's till we meet! To our acquaintance!
Meet—who knows; but fuse in one joint cadence.
With self-provinces unknown to me—
With my whole self, Rainer, all the sea!

Let's not miss each other—drop a card;
Here's to your new sound-recording art!

Stairs in Heaven, downward the Host is pointing . . .
Here is, Rainer, to your new anointing!

With my hand I shelter it from damp.
Past the Rhone and the Rarogne's banks,
Right across that plain and sheer expanse,
This to Rainer—Maria—Rilke's hands.

Bellevue
February 7, 1927

TRANSLATIONS OF "THE PANTHER"
— CRITICAL APPRAISALS

Critiques by Walter Arndt

The taut, seamless perfection of this most famous of the animal poems is thrown into high relief by the misprisions, shortcuts, evasions, and *pis allers* of the translators not born to Rilke's language. Let us not just vaguely "compare" some version but pass them in review one by one, note felicities, and account for errors and lapses of taste that remove them out of aesthetic recognition of the original:

J. B. LEISHMAN

His gaze those bars keep passing is so misted
with tiredness, it can take in nothing more.
He feels as though a thousand bars existed,
and no more world beyond them than before.

Those supply-powerful paddings, turning there
in tiniest of circles, well might be
the dance of forces round a centre where
some mighty will stands paralyticly.

Just now and then the pupil's noiseless shutter
is lifted. — Then an image will indart,
down through the limbs' intensive stillness flutter,
and end its being in the heart.

Line 2: Defect in German; *nichts mehr* 'nothing any more' translated as if it were *nicht mehr* 'no more (of something).' The idea is not that the gaze can't take in anything but bars any more but that it can't take in ANYTHING. Also, meter spoilt by 'nothing more' for, say, 'no more.'
Line 4: Similar trouble with 'more.' Should be 'no world,' not 'no more world.' 'Than before' is padding.
Lines 6, 7: Forces: the plural is a gratuitous fault — *force around* would have solved the spurious metrical dilemma. The rhyming on *where* / *there* and *be* / *-ly* is sadly weak. No further points need be made, though, since line 8 resoundingly disqualifies the whole enterprise.

His vision from the passing of the bars
is grown so weary that it holds no more.
To him it seems there are a thousand bars
and BEhind A thouSAND bars, uh, no world.

The padding gait of flexible strong strides,
that in the very smallest circle turns,
is like a dance of strength around a center
in which stuPEfied a great will, uh, stands.

OnLY someTIMes the curtain of the pupil
soundlessly parts—then an iMAge enTERS,
goes through the "tensioned" stillnes of the limbs—
and in the heart ceaSES to be.

This sample is not so much a failed achievement as a failure to try. A Rilke translation with neither rhyme scheme nor even iambics preserved is simply *hors de concours*. The farcical effect of capitalizing misstressed syllables above is to emphasize that when dealing with Rilke, modernist 'relaxed metrics' are no refuge to translators who haven't the gift of being accurate semantically as well as prosodically.

C. F. MACINTYRE

His sight from ever gazing through the bars
has grown so blunt that it sees nothing more.
It seems to him that thousands of bars are
before him, and behind him nothing merely.

The easy motion of his supple stride,
which turns about the very smallest circle,
is like a dance of strength about a center
in which a mighty will stands stupefied.

Only sometimes when the pupil's film
soundlessly opens . . . then one image fills
and glides through the quiet tension of the limbs
into the heart and ceases and is still.

Line 2: the usual American error of 'nothing more' for 'nothing any more.'
Line 3: the painful collision, phonetic and metric, of 'bars are' should not have been allowed to stand.
Line 4: There is a hole at the end of the line; or does 'merely' stand for an iambic rhyme with 'more'?

Stanza 3: Aside from the helpless impression made by the half and quarter rhymes, 'one image' for 'an image,' 'fills' without object, the spoiler 'and' starting line 3, and the extra 'and is still' at the end mark the translation a failed draft.

JESSIE LEMONT

His weary glance, from passing by the bars,
Has grown into a dazed and vacant stare;
It seems to him there are a thousand bars
And out beyond those bars the empty air.

The pad of his strong feet, that ceaseless sound
Of supple tread behind the iron bands,
Is like a dance of strength circling around,
While in the circle, stunned, a great will stands.

But there at times the pupils of his eyes
Dilate, the strong limbs stand alert, apart,
Tense with the flood of visions that arise,
Only to sink and die within his heart.

Jessie Lemont's is the only version so far that honors the esthetic necessity of the steady binary (usually iambic) pulse without which any imitation is at a hopeless remove from the classic Rilke of the advancing century. Unfortunately, she has bought this assonance at a heavy cost in dilution and departure—losing not only the fine closing image but the vital impact of lines 7 and 8 by a gratuitous syntactic weakness. The third stanza dissolves into fantasy.

STEPHEN MITCHELL

His vision, from the constantly passing bars,
has grown so weary that it cannot hold
anything else. It seems to him there are
a thousand bars, and behind the bars, no world.

As he paces in cramped circles, over and over,
the movement of his powerful soft strides
is like a ritual dance around a center
in which a mighty will stands paralyzed.

Only at times, the curtain of the pupils
lifts, quietly—. An image enters in,
rushes down through the tensed, arrested muscles,
plunges into the heart and is gone.

Here, in a dozen lines, we are asked to accept several dozen failures and gratuitous distortions.

Line 1: "constantly" has been inserted to fill the line; it is worse than superfluous, tripping the iambic flow up with a dactylic foot.

Line 3: the usual little blunder of the non-native: *nichts mehr* is 'nothing any more,' not 'nothing else.'

Line 4: the drugged languor of the stanza is spoiled, from mere ineptitude, by the indecent hop-and-skip of an anapaest. Its rhymes, moreover, are replaced by assonances. Close assonances may be unavoidable second-bests occasionally, but to this pains-faking paraphrast they are neither close nor occasional but part of a cheery what-the-hellitude that Rilke, of all delicate artists, has not deserved. *Er war ein Dichter*, Rilke noted somewhere, *und er hasste das Ungefähre*: "He was a poet, and he hated the approximate."

In the second stanza, the first line has turned trochaic, which is harmless enough; 'over' is rhymed with 'center,' 'strides' with '-lyzed,' which once more testifies to the reverse of genius, i.e., an infinite incapacity for taking pains. Yet in its flawed way, the stanza is reminiscent of Rilke's.

The third stanza produces more assorted lapses, both formal and semantic. In the second line, if Rilke had meant 'quietly' he would have put 'leise,' but he said 'lautlos,' for which 'soundlessly' is a perfect semantic and metric fit; at the end of this line, for Mitchell an image enters 'in'—the type of pervasive American redundancy which produces 'up until,' 'dis-as-sociate' for dissociate, 'off of,' 'equally as,' 'whether or not' for whether, 'can't help but' for can't but, 'infringe "on" a rule' for infringe it, 'expand "on,"' and a hundred others. This image should be entered out. In line 3 of the stanza, Mitchell suddenly loses his footing: The image "rushes down" instead of Rilke's "moves through," then "plunges into the heart" with no textual excuse whatever. He has fortified the artifact, though, by rhyming "pupils" with "muscles," and the supererogatory "in" with "gone."

This Panther is not among the more lifelike specimens of the taxidermist's art. But then Mr. Mitchell, interviewed early in 1988 about his undertaking to translate Laotse into English without knowing Chinese, declared that it was not necessary to know the language of origin to produce a translation.

Critique of Walter Arndt's working draft
by Joel Agee

So wearied from the passing bars of iron
Is now his gaze, it fails to fasten on.
To him a thousand bars seem to environ
The present, and no world to lie beyond.

The supple force of strides which softly enter
That tautest turning of their circling drill
Is like a dance of strength about a center
In which there stands benumbed a mighty will.

But soundless, now and then, the pupil's curtain
Will draw apart . . . An image then is passed,
Pervades the halted limbs with tense alerting,
And in the heart gives out its last.

I am not happy with your version, although it is formally
the most accurate of the lot.

Line 2: "is now his gaze," placed where it is at the end of
the opening clause, sounds like German syntax; it's not nat-
ural in English.

"It fails to fasten on" would mean "der sich an nichts mehr
hält;" it's the sense of *containment* in "halten" that's meant,
or more literally of *holding*, but not of holding on, not of
adherence. Aside from that, "fasten on" sounds like an awk-
ward substitute for "cling," since it's not normally used with-
out an object; that is, one is left dangling in expectation of at
least an implied object *to* which the failing gaze might have
fastened on (such as "to anything"). As the sentence stands,
one imagines that what the gaze fails to fasten onto is the
passing bars, which of course is not the idea.

Lines 3 and 4: "environ / the present" introduces a com-
plicated idea that is not in the original. "Environ" is, in
itself, too abstract a verb for Rilke. "And no world to lie
beyond" takes a troubling liberty with grammar: the plural
seem of line 3 cannot be applied to the singular "world" of
line 4.

Lines 5 and 6: Stripped of adjectives and adverbs, the state-
ment boils down to: "The strides enter the turning of their
drill." There is nothing so complicated, and again, so abstract,
in the German.

Line 10: If there were no need to rhyme or scan, "enters"
would obviously be a much better translation of "geht hinein"
than "is passed," which to my ears has either a medical
(kidney-stones) or military (". . . in review") provenance.

Line 11: Again a different idea from that of the original: In the German, the image *passes through the tense stillness* of the limbs; in your line, the image produces tension in the limbs. Also, "pervades . . . with alerting" is awkward.

Line 12: "Gives out its last" is too dramatic an expiration. "Hört auf zu sein" expresses simple extinction, no more and no less.

The only two successive lines that have the feeling, the sound, and the meaning of the original without any subtraction or addition are lines 7 and 8.

The problem, I think, is that strict fidelity to the form forces you to be semantically "ungefähr" and at the same time too clever, *recherché* instead of plain-spoken, ingenious instead of ingenuous. The artificiality of the rhyme scheme, in Rilke, is beautifully humbled by the simplicity of the diction; in your version, the diction, the tone and gestural manner of the poem, are made artificial by the strictures of the rhyme. I don't think that can be helped, unless you were to sacrifice either the rhyme or the meter or both. Given the need for this unhappy choice, as seems to be the case here, I would dispense with rhyme before meter, since in English, if the rhyming words don't come with an alibi of syntactical innocence or semantic necessity, they immediately look self-conscious and guilty of interloping in important matters that are none of their business ("environ," "drill," and "alerting" are cases in point); and usually they come with unrhymed accomplices that make the entire line suspect. Something is lost with the rhyme, it's true, even a part of the meaning; but it is the most artificial and therefore the most extrinsic part. The poem may or may not bleed without it; I think it is worth trying.

Summarizing, I believe that "form-true" translation of rhymed lyric (as distinct from humorous, narrative, philosophical, etc.) verse rarely succeeds and usually fails, not because the translator lacks talent, skill, or patience, but because for technical reasons it cannot be done. I strongly suspect that this is the case with "Der Panther," at least in English.

Joel Agee's Response to Arndt's New Version

His gaze has been so worn by the procession
Of bars that it no longer makes a bond.
Around, a thousand bars seem to be flashing,
And in their flashing show no world beyond.

The lissom steps which round out and re-enter
That tightest circuit of their turning drill
Are like a dance of strength about a center
Wherein there stands benumbed a mighty will.

Only from time to time the pupil's shutter
Will draw apart: an image enters then,
To travel through the tautened body's utter
Stillness—and in the heart to end.

I didn't get to respond immediately to your new "Panther"
version. It's so much better than the old one—a better English
poem and a better translation—much closer to Rilke's tone.
In fact I find it admirable, and my first reaction was a big grin
of delight and the impulse to eat my words according to
which "it can't be done." But there are two standards, that of
the original and that of the copy. As a fellow translator I
stand with you outside the gates of Eden and want to say to
the man with the keys—especially after reading all the other
versions—"This one is very good, probably as good a version
as there ever will be;" but as a bilingual reader, I am in the
position to take my stand firmly and with very little effort in
the heaven of the German poem—and from this vantage I
still see a few signs of purgatorial strain: "In their flashing
show no world beyond"—compared with the plainness of
the German; "drill"—(as you yourself pointed out); "makes
a bond" still has the adhesive sense of "halten," which I don't
think is the intended meaning, and the secondary implica-
tion of emotional "bonding," which is absent in the original;
"lissom" is close to "geschmeidig" but a much rarer, even
rarefied, word. The "flashing" of the bars is an addition and
as such questionable—but it's so closely involved with the
idea of the bars *blinding* the panther that I don't mind it—and
the half-rhyme "procession / flashing" strikes me as very
good—as do all the rhymes. "Strength" in line 7 is more
accurate than the earlier "force"—lines 7 and 8 seem just
about perfect. And the solution of the last line, in fact the
last stanza, is beautiful.

ANOTHER RENDERING OF "GOING BLIND," WITH COMMENTS

S. Mitchell's rendering of "Die Erblindende":

She sat just like the others at the table.
But on second glance, she seemed to hold her cup
A little differently as she picked it up.
She smiled once. It was almost painful.

And when they finished and it was time to stand
and slowly, as chance selected them, they left
and moved through many rooms (they talked and laughed),
I saw her. She was moving far behind

the others, absorbed, like someone who will soon
have to sing before a large assembly;
upon her eyes, which were radiant with joy,
light played as on the surface of a pool.

She followed slowly, taking a long time,
as though there were some obstacle in the way;
and yet as though, once it was overcome,
she would be beyond all walking, and would fly.

LINE 1: A slightly Germanic word order: "at tea" or "at the table" should normally follow "she sat," unless (a) the translation treats the-others-at-the-table as one unit which the girl "sits like," or (b) Mitchell needs the unorthodox position of "table" for an end rhyme in line 4. The latter may be the case; but what the reader is offered is the "table"/"painful" rhyme, which is not worth even the smallest candle.

LINE 2: The original has "at first it seemed to me"; Mitchell idly puts "but on second glance." There had been no previous glance, for the girl's grasp of the tea-cup was the first thing that called the poet's attention to her. Next, the translator stretches the comfortable and canonical five feet of the meter to a sloppy and needless six; probably inadvertently, for Mitchell is constrained throughout by his equipment to rate the convenience of the prosodically untutored translator above the esthetic identity of the poem.

LINE 3: Mitchell's rhyme-prompted insertion "as she picked it up" is of course gratuitous, but fits in with a minimum of "noise."

LINE 4: Here the extra feet dangled into lines 2 and 3 contrast with a short, four-foot line; deprived of its pith, alas, by the lame "feminine" half-response to the first line's unfortunate "table." "Es tat fast weh" is a comment of casual pathos which seems to call for the iambic taps of "it almost hurt" instead of the mushy six syllables we find here.

LINES 5, 6: The meter here could be called "Modern U.S. Unbuttoned": "it was" in line 5 is tossed into the upbeat of a single iambus, and so is "-ly as" in line 6. This practice caters to post-1940 American metric taste, not to the prosody of Rilke's poetry, and the more it is indulged, the more the resulting "speech rhythms" will have moved away from the esthetic of the original. On the other hand, a strong case can be made by translators like Mitchell (provided they at least fully understand the originals) for "consumer-oriented" translation. The delicate and relatively exotic quiddity of many a Rilkean artifact may be irreproducible eighty years later in a wholly different clime.

LINE 8: The original has "she followed the others closely" (naturally, or she'd lose her bearings); Mitchell has her "moving far behind." This argues quite a primitive defect in his German, as well as an odd lapse in his grasp of a simple situation. "Sie ging den anderen nach" means she followed them, never anything like "she fell behind them." Could the "behind" have been clutched, rather desperately, as a Mitchell rhyme to the "stand" which ends line 5?

LINE 9: "Verhalten" is not "absorbed." Its essence is a sense of inner reserve and tension, self-induced inhibition.

LINES 10, 11, 12: The meter as well as the rhyme scheme fall into complete ruin here, lurching from flawed iambics to trochees and half back, with even sadder birth defects induced by careless abortants like "upon her eyes,which were raDIANT with joy" (for "on her light/lucent eyes, which were glad, external light lay as on a pool."). "Soon, pool, assembly, and joy" are offered the listener to stand for the echoes of gleich, Leuten, freuten, Teich.

STANZA 4: A faulty ticker and a cupronickel ear are at work here once more. The slight collision between "long" and "time" is harmless, though not helpful. But lines 1 and 3 should be rhymed properly, lest in line 1 she take a "long tum." And, at no cost whatever, the silly pothole in the last line should be filled in by putting "past" instead of "beyond."

One cannot but conclude that what Mitchell does is to contort the Rilke poem into as many debasing compromises as his own formidable handicaps require. Perhaps this cruel formula applies to all verse translators; but there surely must be a point where the load of disqualifications causes the vessel to sink below the Plimsoll line. What resulted in the present instance is an undersaturated mess, with stray splinters of Rilke's perfect crystals bobbing sadly in the Mitchell porridge.

THE CIRCUMSTANCES OF THE WRITING OF "INTIMATION OF REALITY"

This brilliant poem of death as a chink of light opening into reality was written in memory of one of Rilke's noble benefactresses. The physical circumstances of its genesis are characteristic of the poet's life, from about age thirty on, as a protégé, house guest *sine die*, and literary mascot of the belletristically inclined noblewomen of central Europe.

In this instance, Alice Faehndrich, the sister of one of Rilke's most generous well-wishers, Louise Countess Schwerin, had invited him to spend the winter of 1907, "with complete freedom to work," at the family villa on Capri. By 1908, his second stay at this fairy-tale retreat—comparable in all but its seclusion to the writers' and artists' studios at Villa Serbelloni on Lake Como—the countess had died. The poem *Todeserfahrung* was written on Capri on the first anniversary of her death and the first six lines of it, without indication of authorship, are found carved on a tombstone in the *Cimitero acattolico*, the island's graveyard for "other denominations." Oddly enough, the stone now marks the grave of the Countess's daughter, Gudrun Baroness Uexküll, who died over sixty years later, and is buried next to her husband on a spot commanding a dazzling picture-postcard view of the Bay of Naples and Mt. Vesuvius. The exquisite hospitality extended to the poet by the châtelaines on Capri, their worshipful solicitude for his working day, and his requital in literary coin are sufficiently typical to be worth relating in some detail. Wolfgang Leppmann in his superb biography, *Rilke: A Life*, Fromm International, 1984, evokes the particular setting on Capri as follows.

Alice Faehndrich, well aware of his need for solitude, allots him the "little rose cottage," which reminds him of the *studio al ponte* of his Roman winter. Again he is lodged in a small, quiet, detached structure in the garden of a villa. All day he can work or stroll as he pleases without being disturbed or disturbing others. For the evening meal he generally repairs to the manor house, the Villa Discopoli in its cocoon of roses and clematis, which is near the Via Tragara and offers a broad view of the Certosa and the sea. There Rilke holds court; there on the long winter evenings he entertains his ladies: the forty-nine-old Alice Faehndrich, née Baroness von Nordeck zur Rabenau; her sixty-four-year-old stepmother, "Frau Nonna," alias Julie Baroness von Nordeck zur Rabenau, née Countess Wallenberg; and the twenty-four-year-old Manon Countess zu Solms-Laubach, whose family he knows from a visit to Darmstadt. He reads to them, writings of his own and poems by Verhaeren and

Hesse's *Peter Camenzind*, and allows them to spoil him. Years later, again as a guest at a noble estate, he ruefully recalls this atmosphere, so oddly compounded of maternal, literary, and erotic elements. "Oh, dear Frau Nonna, enviable as this may be [he is writing from Duino Castle, where no one is about but an old valet and the housekeeper]—it isn't Capri, it isn't Villa Discopoli; what would I not give for the occasional sight of a pair of ladies' hands busy with the almost spiritual labor of knitting or embroidery —quite apart from the fact that there is nobody here who would peel me an apple. That spectacle, and this little favor somehow afforded me strength for years in those days, but it is long used up by now . . " Not for the first time [resumes Leppmann with perhaps undue severity], one is bound to smile at the preciosity of this man who on a magic island in the year 1906 plays Tasso to three titled ladies, and Adam to an apple-proffering Eve, while in the world outside the rail link through the Simplon Tunnel is opened, the international convention banning night labor for women is signed, and the radio telephone is introduced. On the other hand, the sybaritic picture (which he evokes again even after the War in a letter to Nanny Wunderly-Volkert) should not blind us to the sad truth it seeks to cover up. For Rilke is among the people to whom fortune always beckons from a place where they are not. Thus the apple-peeling ladies' hands in Villa Discopoli stand for the elusiveness of a happiness that has come his way now and then in the past, may do again in the future, but is virtually barred from the present (pp. 223–24).

RILKE:
A COMPACT BIOGRAPHY

A Chronicle of Rilke's Life and Writings

1875

René Karl Wilhelm Johann Joseph Maria Rilke born in Prague on December 4. This is also the year of Thomas Mann's birth.

1882

R is put into boys' clothes for the first time upon entering German elementary school at Graben and Herrengasse, where "Bohemian" (Czech) is taught as a foreign language.

1886–91

Years spent in military academies at Vienna-St. Pölten and in Moravia. Though not suited or committed to an army career, he actually earns a distinguished record but leaves two years before the expected graduation with a lieutenancy. For obscure reasons, he later grotesquely exaggerates the "martyrdom" he underwent during those years.

1892

After an abortive trial year at a school of business at Linz, Upper Austria, R is tutored for three years in Prague by high school teachers and passes his high school certificate in 1895. Not interested in the university study his well-to-do uncle, Jaroslav Rilke, is about to finance for him, R is busy writing poetry and prose and seeking contacts with publishers and editors.

1894

R publishes his first book of poems, *Leben und Lieder*, "by René Maria Rilke," in Strassburg. He very understandably disavows this collection later.

1895–96

University study at Prague, then Munich, sponsored by R's uncle with a view to launching him on a career in law, is used by R mainly as a convenient cover and meal ticket for his literary projects. He has decided to give up study for a degree and become a poet and writer. At the turn of 1895–96 he publishes his second collection of poems, a curiously Slavophile tribute to Prague and the Czech home region which he called *Larenopfer*, "Sacrifice to the Lares." A third collection follows in 1896: *Traumgekrönt*, "Dream-Crowned," an indulgence in a new mode which R and others refer to as "mood lyric." Even acknowledging the successive radical changes of poetic taste and tolerance over almost a century, one marvels that R seems to have found it relatively easy to find publishers for cycle after cycle. To the modern reader the quality of his early work might well have buried his name forever.

The year in Munich yields R, besides a rising literary reputation, two very important encounters. He discovers the celebrated Danish psychological realist, Jens Peter Jacobsen, then at the height of an international influence that has since faded. His novels give R an example of calm and authenticity which his neoromantic eccentricity badly needs, and they kindle a lifelong strong interest in Denmark and Scandinavia. This attraction finds expression in some of R's poetry of the best period and especially in the extraordinary prose poem, *The Notebooks of Malte Laurids Brigge*, which combines the Parisian and Danish habitats of his mind.

The second encounter is deeply personal as well as literary. He meets, woos, and soon wins the love of Lou Andreas-Salomé, a critic and essayist of note fourteen years his senior, daughter of a Moscow general, irresistible collector of outstanding minds in the manner of the later Alma Mahler-Gropius-Werfel, close companion of Nietzsche until his lapse into insanity ("she is by far the brightest person I have known"). She acts as R's mentor in worldly and literary matters, and soon as his guide to Russian and Russia, which to the incurable young faddist of vaguely intuited Slavic antecedents reveals itself as the homeland of his spirit: "Russia is forever sunk into the foundation wall of my life." The character of their relationship changes after a few years, but its essence persists; none of R's numerous later patronesses and chatelaines has a remotely comparable influence on his psyche and self-understanding as a man and a poet.

In the autumn of 1897 Lou returns to Berlin-Schmargendorf, and R gives up his fragile student status at Munich and moves to Berlin. He comes in contact almost immediately with two artists maturer than himself, who severely challenge his facile *Stimmungslyrik*: the lyrical cult-hero Stefan George with his sacerdotal solemnity, glib versification, and (to those immune to his virus) ludicrous pretentiousness, and the great sculptor, Auguste Rodin. This year sees the publication of R's fourth collection of poetry, called *Advent*, which in some respects points beyond the mood lyric of the last few years toward the mature elements of *Buch der Bilder*.

1898

On a journey to Florence, R becomes acquainted with a prominent idyllic landscapist and illustrator of the still quite small but modish circle of painters associated with the moor village of Worpswede north of Bremen. He is Heinrich Vogeler, one of, ultimately, many dozen Maxfield Parrish gurus of *fin-de-siècle* German *Jugendstil*. Worse still, Vogeler's style is almost indistinguishable, in his graphic work, from Beardsley in mannerisms, but lacks Beardsley's spicy decadence. R's taste, in painting and poetry, has been swept up from adolescence in the art nouveau wave, which helps to account for the mawkishness, esthetic falsity, and sheer bad taste of most of his early verse.

In the Boboli gardens R happens upon Stefan George, who greets him affably, but soon confides to him his well-founded judgment that R has proceeded too hastily in publishing his verse. They part amicably, but will not meet again.

R accepts Vogeler's invitation to spend Christmas with him in Bremen, and pays his first visit to Worpswede. The little community of painters should be imagined as similar to Rockport, Massachusetts, in the 1920s, where artists rented houses or studios in a "working village" and had no common facilities; in contrast to the present-day MacDowell Colony at Peterborough, New Hampshire, for instance, where accommodation is maintained and allocated by a foundation.

1899

R starts for Russia in April with Lou and her husband for a journey of less than two months. This takes them to Moscow for less than a week, where R meets Lev Tolstoy (in his metropolitan persona), the distinguished painter Leonid Pasternak (the nine-year-old Boris's father), and the celebrated realistic genre painter Ilya Repin. The remaining five weeks are spent in and near St. Petersburg, Lou's native city. The imprint made on R's mind by Russian art and civilization is so strong that, assisted by Lou, he spends the summer in exhaustive study of the language, literature, art, and cultural history of his adopted country, "as if they had to prepare for some dreadful examination" (thus their disappointed hostess, Frieda von Bülow).

In July R is once more invited to stay with Vogeler at his congenial art-craft mansion in Worpswede, "Der Barkenhoff," where he hosts a large circle of writers, including two young artists-friends, Paula Becker, soon to be a famous painter, and Clara Westhoff, the gifted sculptress, whom R will marry a year or two later. As it happens, these meetings are post-poned to the following summer.

Besides progress in Russian studies in anticipation of a second trip, this autumn yields a quantitatively respectable harvest: the cycle "The Tsars" in *Book of Images*, "The Book of Monkish Living," which constitutes the first part of *The Book of Hours*, and *Stories of Our Lord*. To these bestselling Rilkeana of 1899 must be added the inexhaustibly popular *Cornet* and R's dimly fulsome fifth volume of verse, *Mir zur Feier* ("For me to Celebrate with"), with fitting décor by Vogeler.

1900

In May, R embarks on his second Russian pilgrimage, again with Lou but this time without her husband. They do more sightseeing in Moscow, then tour the south, and run into Leonid Pasternak and 10-year-old Boris at Kursk Railroad Station; this meeting is still vivid in Boris's mind a quarter century later, when he and the great poet Marina Tsvetaeva start a correspondence with their childhood idol Rilke—only fifteen years their senior—in the last summer of his life. The travelers decide on an impromptu visit to Lev Tolstoy at Yasnaya Polyana, which yields mainly embarrassment; but R transmutes the vacuous conversation and later gilds the memory of his abortive visit to the Shrine. At Whitsuntide R and Lou go on to marvel at Kiev's famous sanctuaries, take ship down the Dnieper and up the Volga, spend weeks in the country east of Moscow, finally return to St. Petersburg and separate. R works assiduously in libraries and museums. He makes important contacts—later to result in some essays on trends in Russian art—with leaders of the art world like the editors of the leading literary and artistic journal, *Mir Iskusstva*, the art historian and illustrator of Pushkin, Alexandr Benois, and the rising young choreographer Sergey Diagilev. After almost three months, R and Lou arrive back in Berlin in late August, and R goes on to Worpswede the very next day. After an aggregate sojourn of about five months in Russia, his innocence about the desperate social and eco-nomic crisis there, which leads even the most superficial observer to foresee an imminent catastrophe, is as striking as the mind-set which accounts for it: R wallows in the archaic fiction of a patriarchic society of patiently enduring tillers of black soil who labor under the protection of great-souled wolf-hunting magnates and apple-cheeked bibulous squires; choiring monks and even Little Father Tsar round out R's deluded view of Russian life. The sickly, pseudomedieval pietism which informs so many of R's poetic fictions, early and late, including the first part of *Book of Hours,* has clearly infected R's perception of the essential Russia; but the delusion is deliberate. Russia has to be as he wills her to be, or she cannot be his elective home, elective Slav that he fancies himself to be. He keeps her intact as he has shaped her in his fervent *art nouveau* imagination; and while he travels incessantly all over Italy and Spain, North Africa, central Europe and Scandinavia in the years before World War I, he never sets foot in Russia again—as one might hesitate to revisit the site and scenes of an idealized childhood.

R spends late August and September at Vogeler's rebuilt and self-decorated manor, the Barkenhoff, a hotbed of *Jugendstil.* In early October, he rents a house in Worpswede, but abruptly leaves for his Berlin flat and works on more *Book of Images* poems. In December, his third volume of prose is published by the then fledgling publishing house, Inselverlag, later celebrated for outstanding fiction and poetry all over Europe. The book is *Geschichten vom lieben Gott,* and it is well received, probably because the stylized piety and mannered estheticism of these would-be simple-minded morality tales and legends, set in bogus Russian and Italian renaissance settings, found a weakness in European public taste. Both Stefan Zweig and Hofmannsthal briefly wrote in this vein; so did the great Russians, Soloviëv and Blok, and even the early Thomas Mann. Neither R nor Lou betray any awareness of the Russian literary symbolists or acmeists who dominated the *fin de siècle.* But since R has just returned from his visits to Russia and Tolstoy, it is not far-fetched to lay some of the blame for at least the Russian-flavored "tales of our Lord" upon those products of Tolstoy's self-reductionist old age, his "stories for children and simple people." Although R's *Lieber Gott* tales appeared before his stay in Sweden in 1904, one can't help comparing them with Selma Lagerlöf's once famous *Kristuslegender,* so similar in tone.

In the middle of the same month of December, R undergoes a profound existential crisis, assailed by disbelief in the caliber of his talent and his ability to maintain himself, let alone a family. His unconscious "good-by to all kitsch," the dashing of the *Jugendstil* scales from his eyes, and the arresting break-through of his true gift to the heights of *Neue Gedichte* should probably be assigned to those weeks of his inner reckoning.

A projected third journey to Russia is tacitly canceled: a sign of his withdrawal from Lou Salomé and his headlong commitment to the young artists of the Worpswede colony (not one of whom was a writer, incidentally). He is especially attracted to Paula Becker and the tall, dark, severely beautiful young sculptress, Clara Westhoff. Staying at the Barkenhoff, R rather tries the patience of the Vogelers and startles the honest peat-cutters by continuing to feed the Russian bats in his belfry, sporting a wispy beard and walking about "in Tartar boots" and a *rubashka* ("with his shirttail hanging out!").

In early December, at a party arranged by Lou, R meets the leading naturalist dramatist, Gerhart Hauptmann. They impress each other strongly. Hauptmann sends R a signed copy of his just-completed play, *Michael Kramer*, and R responds by an elaborate critique of the play and, later, an inscribed copy of *Buch der Bilder*—one of perhaps two of his works he still stands by at this point. Clearly ready for a new phase in his life and art, he seeks and finds an emotional home in the company and the studios of the three noted Worpswede painters, Modersohn, Mackensen, and Vogeler; but he finds especially comforting the company of Paula and Clara, with whom he is linked in a harmonious *sentiment-à-trois*.

R spends the winter months of 1900–1901 back in Berlin, preparing for the third Russian pilgrimage and working on articles and essays intended to help launch modern Russian art in Germany. He writes Clara almost daily letters to Worpswede, but still seems attracted also to Paula.

1901

In January, Clara and Paula, who is now engaged to marry Modersohn, come to Berlin on a visit. The next month, R receives a missive from Lou that is not so much a dismissal as a stern declaration of independence. She has spent too many years guiding R and propping up his ego—partly for fear that his unstable temperament might lead him to suicide or dementia; she has now found her way back to the real self of her youth and (she is turning forty) will serve her own artistic gifts and goals, alone and emotionally untrammeled. On a gentler final note, she offers him refuge, as before, in case of suicidal crises or serious illness. Lou seems to divine, or gather from certain changes in R's behavior, that he is about to bind himself to a younger woman, but she doesn't mention Clara. It becomes clear in his later life that R's creative impulses have been so conditioned and catalyzed by the intellectual intimacy with Lou over the four years of their liaison that he all but ignores Lou's plea for independence. She remains his confidante and must be thought of as his wife in as true a sense as Clara, let alone anyone else on R's later Don Juan roster.

On April 28 R and Clara get married and settle at Westerwede, at the edge of the same moorland as Worpswede. A daughter, Ruth, R's only child, is born to them in mid December. Both parents work at their professions but cannot make ends meet. As R longed for Russia, so Clara has long dreamt of moving to Paris to work with her idol Rodin, who had been one of her teachers.

1902

The Rilkes dissolve their household at Westerwede and move to Paris, where Clara re-enlists as a pupil of Rodin's, while R (who will be engaged by the irascible old genius as his secretary a few years later) is at a loose end. R's penury (and his curiously isolationist concept of the marital relation, to be cited below) even at this early stage presage the end of the bourgeois marriage he had entered into with much joy and élan. His books, until the astonishing bestsellerdom of the *Cornet* from 1905 to the present, yield almost no royalties. The allowance from his southern family, which has been his financial mainstay, is about to be cut off. He is forced to cast about desperately for editorial or reviewing jobs. It is here, or soon after, that the peripatetic second half of his life begins. Overrich in affluent patronesses and besotted young women, he is essentially bare of wholly congenial support, uxorial or other. Clara and he drift apart without a breach or a lessening of mutual solicitude; the following excerpts from R's letters show graphically that Clara for all her devotion to her art wants to be more of a wife than R permits her to be; while his main concern in a marriage is the strict preservation of either partner's artistic insulation and ego integrity. By early spring of 1902 R has made up his mind to leave Westerwede with Clara and give up their first and only household. He writes to Arthur Holitscher, a friend from Prague days:

No, nothing has turned up, that is, no external thing, just a resolve: we are moving to Paris in the autumn. My wife has worked there before under Rodin, as you know, and I consider it important right now for her art (of which I expect magnificent things!) to be near the great master. And I too hope for a great deal of help for my Russian work and everything else. Here I often lack the necessary wherewithal, libraries etc. . . . . Over there I expect an abundance of everything, plus solitude. . . . I hope my wife may get some sort of stipend, in which case I am confident I'll find some way to subsist.

My wife will rent a studio, I a furnished room; and so we'll each live entirely for our work, without the pretext of a "household."[1]

With dubious authority, R implies that he speaks for Clara when he writes to Friedrich Huch, his novelist friend, "By now we have made up our minds, painfully enough, to dissolve our little household, because it turned out that this so-called household was a third person sitting at our table and taking from our plates what we meant to eat. The decision enabled each of us to do a better job living for his/her work; for the idea of our marriage had been that either of us should be of greater help to the other's self and work."

Clara's views on this topic are unrecorded.

In a letter over ten years later to Sidonie Nádherný, a friend who has just sat for a terracotta statuette by Clara, R alludes to the friendly divorce he and Clara have agreed upon and offers this revealing analysis of the conflict between the partners' natures and needs—never mentioning in this context the crucial fact of his chronic indigence and lack of husbanding skills (in every sense of the ambiguous word):

there we all stand (who doesn't?) with our giving of ourselves, with our need to love, and where we exert it no good comes of it—and where we are loved, it confines us. There is a lot of the young girl in Clara, hence, time and again, a lot of longing for a woman's life; and yet, when she subjugates herself she immediately turns disciple rather than wife, more of the pupil and adherent, and for that matter not in the strongest meaning of these but in the mode of surrender and imitation. That is why I don't believe that she had it in her to stand by someone's side as a wife: giving herself to another's life doesn't leave her strong but pliant, she mirrors instead of forming a counterpart. Even if her lot had been quite different, as these days she sometimes thinks it should have been, meaning a real full-scale marriage, many children: things would in no way have been easier for her or less ambivalent. That she happened upon me, of course, was a special hardship, since I was unable to foster properly either the artist in her or her urge for fulfillment as a wife. The farther and more thoroughly I withdraw from life, the better, I suspect, will it be for her. I fully understood her suggesting divorce eighteen months ago, and that it didn't come about was due only to some external obstacles. . . .

That artistic work and normal living are ultimately an either-or proposition everyone discovers in his time, we know; but for a woman the choice may well entail an unequalled pain and departure.

What with the Rilkes' different religions and citizenships, divorce proceedings prove too costly and time-consuming, and the marriage is never formally dissolved.

1. This letter excerpt, and those following, are translations by the author from the general collection of Rilke's *Letters*, edited by Ruth Sieber-Rilke and Carl Sieber, Insel-Verlag, Leipzig, 1930–1933.

Rilke's letters are strewn with brilliant aphorisms and bon mots—a facet of his genius that has been largely overlooked. One that could have originated with Voltaire or Lichtenberg and is germane to the above context is found in a letter, soon after his marriage, to the poet E. v. Bodman. It illustrates R's ideological obtuseness to Clara's simple need to be loved and find the happiness of intimacy in marriage, "It doesn't occur to anybody to demand of an individual that he be 'happy'; but let one get married, and everyone is amazed if he isn't." His work with and on Rodin produces, inter alia, a pithy apothegm one is tempted to look up in La Rochefoucault: "Fame is the aggregate of all misconceptions that gather about a new name."

1903

Life in Paris is uncongenial and oppressive to R, though conducive later to his greatest prose achievement by far, the *Malte* notebooks, that awe-inspiring poetic record of inner-city desolation and squalor. He is busy with a monograph on Rodin, whom he idolizes as a modern Michelangelo. This illustrated book, which combines art criticism with biographic matter and personal memoirs, is published in Berlin in March. With his monograph on Worpswede and its artists, this will make the second of R's sizeable and successful works of non-fiction.

R spends the summer at Worpswede and Oberneuland near Bremen, Clara's family home, then travels in Italy, staying mainly in Rome. Clara, of course, has to stay with little Ruth. Also, not only is her studio not itinerant like R's, but travel *en deux* is evidently considered impractical and unaffordable.

1904

R spends almost the first half of the year in Rome (Villa Strohl-Fern). But Scandinavia, almost as much as Russia five years earlier, has now captivated R's imagination. The influence of the great novelist Jens Peter Jacobsen and, possibly, Ibsen and Strindberg, is evident, for R has been writing plays for many years, not without some success. The figure from *The Notebooks* . . . of the young Danish expatriate in Paris, Malte Laurids Brigge, and numerous poems of 1905 and later testify to the establishment of another surrogate literary home for R in Denmark and the Swedish core-land of Skåne. R's search for a cultural habitat, not to say "fatherland," clearly started in his adolescence, when the Bohemian mi-

nority cultures, the German or the Czech, were too paro-
chial for his questing spirit, and Austrian too exclusive, and
the metropolitan German (with many exceptions) too vulgar
and militaristic. First Russia, then France, then Scandinavia
lure him with the charm of a European spirit that is sturdily
autochthonous and yet cosmopolitan, under whose aegis a
European artist can live and create without national com-
mitment. It has not been sufficiently noticed that after Ren-
aissance times a true Europe existed only in the works and
interchanges of her liberal artists from Petersburg to Paris
and Scandinavia to the Mediterranean in the first quarter of
the 20th century; and a truly European identity may not
exist again before the next century.

The winter of 1904/1905 is spent by the Rilkes in the
surrogate home of their brittle marriage, at the Westhoffs in
Oberneuland. *The Lay of the Love and Death of the Cornet
Christof Rilke* is published, destined to be the hardy peren-
nial of juvenile Rilke *Schwärmerei*.

1905 and 1906

The following chronological itinerary is supplied, not for
the intrinsic interest of any particular vector of R's waterbug
skiddings during those years, but to show the frenzy of peri-
patetic self-display (for badly needed honoraria and to put
himself in the way of noble sponsors, almost invariably fe-
male and *d'un certain age*) which for R filled much of the
pre-war decade. It will be noted that the only prolonged in-
tervals between wanderings are the months he was able to
spend in a salaried position as Rodin's secretary, some of the
time in close proximity to Clara, Rodin's more and more
highly valued pupil.

This two year sample of an essentially homeless artist's
life will make it unnecessary to go into similar detail again.

The spring months of 1905 find R, subsidized, at the snob-
bish "Weisser Hirsch" resort at Dresden; briefly in Berlin;
May and some of June at Worpswede; the summer weeks
following at Göttingen, Berlin, the Harz, Kassel, Marburg;
August at Friedelhausen Manor, one of his free hostelries of
these years; early September at Darmstadt, Godesberg; mid-
dle of September for six weeks lodging with Rodin at Meudon
near Paris; October through November at Cologne, Dresden
(lecture), Prague (lecture), Leipzig, Cologne; the second half
of December at Oberneuland.

(Publication of *The Book of Hours*.)

1906

Until the middle of May, lodging with Rodin at Meudon again; February: Elberfeld [Wuppertal] (lecture); March: Berlin, Hamburg (lecture), Worpswede; March: in Prague for father's burial; late March: Berlin (lecture); middle May: move into new lodgings in Paris, last reunion there with Paula Modersohn-Becker in the last year of her life; her unfinished portrait of him; first half of August: Belgium, second: Bad Godesberg; September: Friedelhausen Manor; October through November: Berlin; December: at the Schwerins' villa on Capri.

1907

R's beatific working vacation on Capri (see commentary to his poem *Todeserfahrung*, p. 169) is extended to almost six months, then complemented by six weeks in Rome and Naples at his own expense. That summer in Paris he encounters the art of Cézanne. It impresses him powerfully, and he very shrewdly connects it with Paula Modersohn's use of grainy color and stylized figuring.

Publication of *Neue Gedichte* (first part), the unsurpassed harvest of R's genius.

1908

Six further weeks are spent on Capri this spring, followed by a few days in Rome and Florence. He briefly moves into a new place in Paris, then into the later famous Hotel Biron, where Clara lives, too, and Rodin rents a whole floor. It eventually becomes the Rodin Museum.

Der neuen Gedichte anderer Teil—The New Poems, Part Two—is published.

1909

In a new departure, R spends a month in the Provence around Avignon.

1910

Some first and some last encounters: R's last journey to the Czech (Teutonic: "Bohemian") homeland, quite overlaid in his mind by two or three later *Wahlvaterländer* (elective homelands); his last stay in Oberneuland; his first view of the modest semifeudal masonry of Duino, one of the spare "castles" of Princess Marie von Thurn und Taxis, where the first two of the elegies he prized so highly would originate some ten years later; and finally, a trip to North Africa, ending in Egypt, where Clara, as it happened, had preceded him on a journey of her own.

The fruit of R's prose endeavors of the years in France, combining his harrowing Paris experiences and an imaginary childhood in a Danish manor-house, is published under the title *The Notebooks of Malte Laurids Brigge*. This, the peak of his prose work, must be placed next to *Neue Gedichte*, which holds the corresponding premier rank in his poetic output.

1911–12

Five years after the deeply mourned loss of Paula Modersohn-Becker, R has his last encounter with the now-admired, now ridiculed regent of German *Jugendstil*, Heinrich Vogeler. This is the epilogue of the Worpswede era of R's life.

The last ten weeks of the year are spent at Duino castle, R's first stay there. It is extended to early May, 1912, and resumed in late October. In August, the "Marienleben" cycle, a throwback to the hail-Maryish variety of expressionism of a decade before, is completed with an injection of fifteen new poems dubiously superior to the rest.

1913–14

Marienleben is published. Throughout this year and half of the next, the rising jingoism in Europe and the multiple needless crises gathering momentum toward war are disbelieved or ignored by R and most of his literary friends—who are Europeans, not "patriots," in a way not seen again after 1914. R spends the early spring of 1913 in Paris, and the summer traveling in Germany. He remains in Paris until past the assassination crisis of June, 1914, when the Austro-Hungarian declaration of war (or possibly vagrant impulses of his own) make him amble back, first to Leipzig and Munich, very much later to Vienna for military service (1916). His utility as a military person striking even the Austrian Army as negligible (though he had done so well as a cadet thirty years earlier), he is made to serve only the first six months of 1916 in and near Vienna, and is then discharged, with some bemusement, back to Munich.

1918

R meets for the last time with Clara and their daughter Ruth in their Munich apartment. Clara and he had been in close touch, despite their technical separations, not only in

Oberneuland and in Paris but also in Munich, where both maintained apartments for years.

1919

R moves to Switzerland—Geneva, Zurich, Soglio, and Locarno—possibly because Switzerland is almost the last refuge of the cosmopolitan and pacifist Europe of the pre-war era.

1921–22

What turns out to be his last steady abode is arranged for R at the Château de Muzot near Sierre on the Rhône in the Swiss Alps. Here he completes both the ten unrhymed *Duino Elegies* (only two of which actually took shape at the eponymous retreat) and the fifty-five *Sonnets to Orpheus*—the two works on which, to many critics and some readers, the reputation of his forties rests.

1923

R's leukemia, undiagnosed almost to the end, prompts him to commit himself to sanatorium stays near Beckenried and, at the end of the year, Val-Mont sur Territet in the Wallis.

The *Elegies* and *Sonnets* are published.

1924

After much travel through Switzerland, R ends up where he began the year, at Val-Mont Sanatorium. Even more troubled about his state of health than he seems himself, Clara comes to visit him at Muzot.

1925

As if trying to deny his increasing frailty, R stubbornly maintains his headquarters at Muzot and embarks upon an, if anything, even more ambitious itinerary than the year before: Paris, Milan, Bern, Ragaz, Meilen, with rest stops at Muzot. Late November finds him at Val-Mont. (His physician later revealed that R in two years of treatment had never so much as asked the nature of his illness or the prognosis. The reticence of the doctor is as arresting as the protective magic invoked by the patient.)

1926

After the first five months in semi-confinement at Val-Mont, R spends several weeks at various resorts around Lake

Geneva, ending at Lausanne and Sierre. By December, he is back at Val-Mont, terribly weakened; on the 29th he dies, and is buried four days later at Raron, Wallis, under his chosen epitaph about rose petals as eyelids.

Rilke's last summer yielded one of his most interesting letter exchanges, totally neglected until recently by the German biographers: his correspondence (brought about by Leonid and Boris Pasternak) with one of Russia's most original and distinguished poets, Marina Tsvetaeva. When she realized that her last letter in December had not reached him alive, she ignored his parting (with his assumed full cognizance and consent) and wrote him the most remarkable epistolary poem of the entire exchange.

SELECTED LIST OF WORKS CONSULTED

Fuerst, Norbert, *Rilke in seiner Zeit*. Frankfurt, 1976.

Grimm, Reinhold, *Von der Armut und vom Regen: Rilkes Antwort auf die soziale Frage*. Königstein/Ts., 1981.

Hamburger, Käte, *Rilke: Eine Einführung*. Stuttgart. 1975.

Jastrun, Mieczysław, *Rainer Maria Rilke: Poezje*. Kraków, 1974.

Leppmann, Wolfgang, *Rilke: Sein Leben, seine Welt, sein Werk*. Bern u. München, 1981.

Mason, Eudo C., *Rainer Maria Rilke: Sein Leben und sein Werk*. Göttingen, 1964.

Pettit, Richard, *Rainer Maria Rilke In und Nach Worpswede*. Worpswede, 1983.

Pfeiffer, Ernst, ed., *Rainer Maria Rilke, Lou Andreas-Salomé, Briefwechsel*. Zürich und Wiesbaden, 1952.

Schnack, Ingeborg, *Rainer Maria Rilke: Chronik seines Lebens und seines Werkes*. Two vols. Frankfurt, 1975.

Schoolfield, George C., *Rilke's Last Year*. University of Kansas Publications, 1966.

Schwarz, Egon, ed., *Zu Rainer Maria Rilke*. Stuttgart, 1983.